Seva
selfless service
The Memoir Of A Modern Day Yogi
by Sistashree (Regina French)

Sistashree (Regina French)

The Memoir Of A Modern Day Yogi
by Sistashree (Regina French)

Copyright © 2016 by Author

ISBN No. 978-1-5136-0876-1

Published and Printed by:

Grafiprint Pvt Ltd. (Div. WQ Judge Press)

97, Residency Road, Bangalore 560 025

In Loving Memory of my Grandmother Mrs. Lallie Barton

THANKS

for this journey.

Also:

Pam, Cherrye, William-Charles, Calvin and Derek 'Doc' Wise.

You are forever in my heart.

I DEDICATE THIS BOOK TO

My wonderful, patient, loving children Zawndra and her family, Nicole and her Boo - you are always in my heart;

My sisters and brothers - we are "best friends forever";

My mother and her siblings who were the best role models anyone could ever ask for and My Family, Neighbors and Friends from Comanche County, Oklahoma and the AME Church in Lawton, which is still the Center for Social Change and Justice.

A special dedication:

GOD AND GURU I SALUTE YOU

CONTENTS

FOREWORD

In this inspiring and easy to read book, Sistashree shares her life experiences in seeing the Sacred in everything.

In her many roles as a daughter, sister, wife, mother, musician and yoga teacher, Sistashree has allowed us a glimpse of her path towards yoga, beyond the poses and the breath to embrace yoga in all that we do.

Whether you are a yoga teacher, or an aspiring yoga student, you will be inspired by "SEVA".

Eileen Hall
YOGA MOVES
Sydney, Australia.

ACKNOWLEDGEMENT

My sincere thanks to the following people for their inspiration, assistance and patience with this project. They actually made it *happen*.

Mrs. Lallie Barton "Momma" my grandmother because she told me the stories and the secrets that made us a loving strong family - a tight community of seekers and believers, who walked in the light and the Grace of God.

Sri K. Pattabhi Jois, Guruji, for taking me on this wonderful Journey from Darkness to Light and his family for their continued guidance.

Ms. Gay Walley, for the many hours of coaching and reading the album covers and compiling information on the artist and music that we both love so much and for helping to create the road map for this book.

Karen Goode, who encouraged me to do the project and kept reading and talking to me all the way through it.

Brianna Hyneman, who gave me lots of good advice and kept reading and commenting and saying "yes you should do this".

Ganjifa Raghupathi Bhatta, for the beautiful art work and continued inspiration. I feel so BLESSED!

Mr. Christopher Hilderbrandt, for the hours of reading and writing the Sanskrit Verses.

Sri Aruna Devi Naresh, for the many hours of reading, editing and arranging the Sanskrit text.

Mr. Rohan Jayawardene, my friend and husband, for his patience in reading and rereading the manuscript and assisting with the book layout and editing. I am forever grateful.

Sri Charlot Kryza, Hong Kong for the many hours of listening and helping me with editing and proofing - you have such great ideas.

Jenny Clayton, UK, thanks for your patience in reading, editing and encouragement.

Mr. Randy Rathnayake, Teacher, St Benedicts College, Colombo for the many hours of editing.

Thanks to the Kumars, Hawaii, for introducing me to Yoga and meditation.

Thanks to all of my students for encouraging me to make those early recordings, and asking me to share my life story.

Thanks to Sister Pearl, the choir director of the greater Pentecostal Church of God and Christ in Tacoma Washington and the members of the Mass and Junior Choirs.

Dhyan Yogi Meditation group in Boston and Gujarat - some of the best chanters I have ever come across. I am so blessed.

John Burton, thank you for being one of the first pioneers of Yoga in Public schools in America.

All the rickshaw drivers, the taxi drivers, the housekeepers, the cooks and the ironing wallah on the streets of India, for sharing their stories with me about life and the many intricate layers of reality in this ancient yet modern place.

Namaste

INTRODUCTION

SEVA, Selfless Service, My life as a Modern Day Yogi

I believe that all life is Spiritual.**
All life is Sacred.**

My journey began in Oklahoma known for its mystical plains.

My childhood was filled with the pain of Segregation and Discrimination.

A young life punctured by random attacks of the Ku Klux Klan.

I remember the birth of the Civil Rights Movement and the death of the great Reverend Dr. Martin Luther King Jr.

I am from a military family. We traveled a lot.

I spent most of my High School years living in Hawaii, where I began to follow the disciplines of the *Sacred Path Of Yoga*.

In the late 1960s I moved to San Diego, California, to attend college but my real learning, growth and development came from local *Neighborhood and Community Service Centers for Social Change and Justice.*

This is where I was introduced to the idea of SEVA - selfless service.

This was the beginning of a life dedicated to *community service and yoga*.

The path of *selfless service*, the discipline of *yoga/meditation* and the heart and soul of Motown nourished my soul so that I could continue to:
Live, Love, Learn and Dance in this magnificent River called Life.

Sistashree, Bangalore 2016

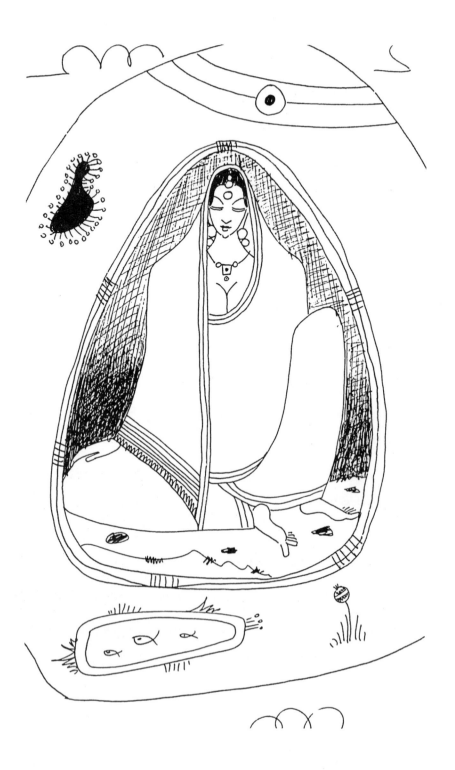

ASANA

मातृ देवो भव ।
पितृ देवो भव ।
आचार्य देवो भव ।
अतिथि देवो भव ।

Mātru devo bhava.
Pitru devo bhava.
Acharya devo bhava.
Atithi devo bhava.

Treat your mother like a God.
Treat your father like a God.
Treat your teacher like a God.
Treat your guests like Gods.
—Taittiriya Upanishad

स्थिरसुखमासनम् ।
Sthirasukhamāsanam.

The seat is stable and comfortable. Building a strong healthy
body, the beginning of the interior journey. —Yoga Sutra

When I think back, the key to a happy childhood could almost be represented by the practice of *Asana*. According to the Ancient scholars of Yoga, Asana is described as a sitting position that is firm and relaxed for extended periods of time. Asana is the third limb of classical Raja Yoga and in today's world, asana practice is the study of postures; postures that strengthen and build the immune system, prevent illness and prepare the body, mind and spirit to sit for long periods to enable one to explore the interior world. The interior journey puts us in touch with our heart and our true self.

A loving childhood that offers strength and guidance does much the same. A childhood full of people who make you smile and who care about your well-being definitely builds a solid foundation for inner calm and the ability to "sit with oneself" for long periods. A childhood that shows you love, action and devotion can prepare you to have the peace of mind to begin a life that is lived from your heart. Where I came from, as difficult as my childhood was in many ways, it is where I unknowingly began my practice of Asana.

That doesn't mean I didn't run away and create a whole different life from the one I was born into, but I went into that new life with Asana in my soul.

My journey began in the summer on August 1, 1952, in Lawton, a small town in Comanche County in the south-western part of Oklahoma. I was an army brat - Oklahoma, West Germany, Tacoma, Washington and Hawaii. Army brat sounds like a pejorative term but, in reality, the benefits of being born into this structured community are many. The men were always off working and the women either worked and tended the children, or kept house and tended the children.

On an army base, everyone got to know one another. There were excellent military schools, the PX - Post Exchange, for shopping, the Commissary for food, household supplies, and seeing your friends or their parents was just a hop, skip, and jump away. Our home was just north of Fort Sill Army Base in Oklahoma. Founded in August 1901 when the last of the native American Territories in Oklahoma were opened for white settlement. Lawton is now the third largest city in Oklahoma, which demonstrates how much the military can boost a local economy.

I think of childhood as the time of being little shamans. When we are children, it is very easy for the conscious and the unconscious mind to exist in altered states. Within those altered states, we, as children, experience the fusion, or the coming together, of the real and the surreal worlds. We are very playful with our thoughts and experience extreme levels of joy without being referred to as eccentric or crazy. People usually say, "what the heck, they are just kids being kids". We often sense the world around us and all of its mysterious ways and constantly express a wonder, freedom and level of mysticism that we somehow loose as we grow. For example, when we were kids, the elders used to tell us to lay flat in the grass on our backs, gaze at the tip of the nose, now focus that gaze, now let the eyes relax beyond the gaze and you will 'see forever'.

3

In the practice of yoga, there is a pose called Savasana or Corpse Pose. Many consider it one of the most important of all yoga poses because the goal is total relaxation:

You lie flat on your back, let your legs relax out to the side, relax the arms with the palms of the hands facing up, you relax the head from side to side then allow it to rest naturally, breath long deep breaths, lengthen the spine and the whole body as much as you can, soften your eyes and focus your gaze at the tip of your nose. Still your mind by listening to the breath and allow yourself to concentrate, allow yourself to meditate.

When we were kids, all we knew was that if we lay flat on the grass on our backs and gazed at the tip of our nose, we would see forever. We would lie there, just breathing softly gazing at the tip of the nose. That focused gaze (looking past the tip of the nose) was a lot like focusing on the *dristi*, in the practice of yoga. Each asana in the practice of Yoga has a dristi - a place where the gaze falls when you are in the pose; so it is a focused gaze. The mind is active at first and then slowly we began to experience 'quiet' and somehow, even as children, we knew and understood that this was good.

Just the simple idea of 'seeing forever' sent chills and thrills up my spine, and being from a small town like Lawton, it was exciting. I mean .... come on, the hip spots in Lawton were the Piggly Wiggly Grocery Store, the neighborhood church, and the Chat and Chew community center and bar. But when we lay in that field and looked out onto the flat landscape we could smell its rich soil, and it created a mystical magic that tingled the soul.

When I was a kid, we sensed that the people around us were tribal, they followed ancient customs. We knew that they were farmers who touched

4

and felt the soil, they came to this land at different times, but they had all learned the secrets of living by the sun and the moon, honoring the earth, seeing it as God.

We were a huge family - and the women were the center. My Grandmother is still there. She likes to remind me when I call, almost every- day, that she is 100 years old, or thereabouts. "In the old days, we depended on the White people at City Hall to make the records (of course we were all born at home)" she recounts, "so sometimes they would record it right, sometimes they wouldn't. We wound up with dates that are sometimes off by a little; it was all according to how they felt the day you went there. So I am," she repeats, "100 or thereabouts".

My Grandmother played a major part in my life as a child, she was my mother's mother and we all called her Momma. But there were others that shaped me; my great-grandmother, Grandma Peyton, my mother and my aunts. Momma had five beautiful children, my mother being one and they were all striking in their own way. That part of the country produced a lot of mixed race people.

There were various combinations of African-American and Native American mixtures - Cherokee, Comanche, Seminole, and Black, with high cheek bones, medium brown-colored eyes, and thick coarse hair. Girls are tall and shapely and the guys are truly tall, black and handsome.

Momma was a domestic for many years and then worked for the Federal Government as a cashier on the Fort Sill military base, and Grandpa was a day worker. Grandpa worked wherever there was work - he went out each morning around sunrise and came back at sunset. That is just how it was done back then. Everybody worked and worked hard. Back in those days, men went out in the morning and worked all day as carpenters, painters, electricians, and plumbers as well as toiling in the fields and factories.

My mother gave birth to six girls and three boys. Seven of us were born when we lived in Oklahoma, and my uncle, Big Junior, came home to celebrate each new child with lots of laughter. The food was always special and delicious.

My uncles were not much of a daily presence. When I was very young, they both left for college on football scholarships, to *Langston University*. They were good people with strong personalities and caring hearts. Big Junior was college-educated, and supervised the school maintenance department in Bakersfield, California, until he retired. His son also attended university on a football scholarship and is a school principal in the Bakersfield school district. Thanks to the advances of Civil Rights movements, by his generation, more positions were available to more African-Americans.

The second uncle, Henry Ji moved to the outskirts of Chicago after his studies, and worked for the Urban League until he retired. Both of these men were positive male role models whose spirits I salute to this day.

My grandfather and my uncles could fix anything. They were hard-working people who had it ingrained in them, and passed on to us the importance of not taking anything for free, to live right, to honor family and follow the rules, and in the 1950s there were a lot of rules to follow.

We were cautioned as children not to look at White people unless they are for some reason addressing you. Not knowing these rules cost many a person their life. *We shall never* forget the murder of *Emmett Till* at the age of 14, on August 28, 1955 (a child being a child) in Mississippi. Till was visiting his mother in Mississippi when he was kidnapped and brutally murdered by white men for supposedly whistling at a White woman in a store.

Our family lived in a big white house and Grandma Peyton lived next door to us. Grandma Peyton was something to see. She weighed no more than eighty pounds soaking wet, with her clothes and shoes on. She was fire and lived by the word and one thing for sure, she 'best not' catch you washing clothes or doing any type of work on Sunday 'cause she called it "the Lord's day", and we were to keep it holy. Grandma Peyton could make some noise for a little itty-bitty woman. She wore a cotton bonnet on her head, a big ol' prairie skirt, and a long-sleeved blouse; the epitome of Oklahoma, right out of the picture books. She rose with the sun and worked all day, hot or cold. She made her soaps, cookies and tea cakes, gathered her eggs and sold all these items in a little cart each day. I will never forget that big black cast iron pot that she fired up outside in her back yard to make soap.

Grandma Peyton's life was pure. She spent her life in service to God, family, and community. She was a simple working class lady and an elder, a *spirit warrior* who served her community and her church. She fed the hungry, cared for sick mothers and children, helped the needy and the elderly, and offered a cup of tea and her ear to those who needed to be heard. Grandma Peyton's devotion to God and her desire to do service for others was inspiring. When I read about Lord Hanuman's devotion to Lord Ram, tears of joy came from my heart as I remember Grandma Peyton.

She said to me, "See with your heart, listen with your heart, that is where love is, that is where God lives", as she touched her heart, looked at me and said, "touch your heart, baby, feel God". I hear those words every time I see someone touch their heart and lower their head. I think about Grandma Peyton and I know that love is real. I can remember her wrapping her arms around me and the heat from her heart warming my soul. She was little, yet strong, and so connected to all of the beautiful things on this planet. Like the prairie lands of Oklahoma, her soul will be a part of the landscape forever. Grandma Peyton was both art and melody.

Grandma Peyton insisted that we go to church on Sundays, to the *African Methodist Episcopal Church* - yes, the AME Church. The Free African Society gave birth to the African Methodist Episcopal Church in 1787 to *protest* racism and segregation in existing churches that forced Blacks to sit in a separate section. The AME Church, which was established on sociological rather than theological reasons, sponsored the second Black independent university and numerous colleges and seminaries. The choir sounded mediocre to me, but across the street was the Baptist Church, with the better choir and I always sat near the window so I could hear that choir raise their voices and sing out around us. As I listened, my soul filled with joy, and like my great-Grandma Peyton, I was touched by all things sublime in this life.

Thinking back to when I was a child, my attachment to music was very similar to my love and commitment to Yoga, which in today's Yoga jargon would be termed as my *practice*. Music was where the joyful, hopeful, spiritual part of me lived.

Music was a constant element of our home-life in those formative years. My mother loved to sing and she had music playing all the time. We had one of those old record players that played 78's and, at that time, we also listened to *AM radio*. There were certain time slots when Black music was played, so we always kept our radios close and listened, waiting for whatever was new. We may not have been in New York City, but if those musicians or those songs came up in conversation, we wanted to be able to answer "Yes, HEARD THAT!!!"

In essence, my childhood was a fusion of *spirit warriors*, medicine men and women, and the Black Church. The Black Church - I should say *The Great Black Church*, the seed of American music. For me it represented *the hope for a better life*. In my soul I always felt that sound in any form, but particularly music, seemed like something very basic, it felt like a fundamental element of life, simply because of how it made me feel. Music was the source of all things good - love happiness, joy and peace.

By the early 1970s I recognized and felt in my heart that I had begun to walk on a particular path. I was extremely clear that some of the answers to life's most important questions were about to be revealed.

During my time at University I listened to music daily, like most students. One day my roommate Rose came into our small room, saying we must listen to this album.

OK who is the artist? I asked
I take one look at the cover and immediately start screaming
Because, it is Bill Withers "Live at Carnegie Hall"

He is one of my favorite musicians.

Live At Carnegie Hall has no fillers. It is music that heals and thrills the soul, it is like yoga, it connects the body, mind and spirit.

It was 1973. *Grandma's Hands*, the fourth track on the album, lasted approximately five minutes - changed my life. It starts with dialogue where Mr. Withers poetically expresses his love for his grandma. He recounts being given the job of caring for her and how that was "a hip job 'cause the only place grandma ever went was to church". At one point in the dialogue he stops and says, "I just love that old lady". He tells a few jokes and goes on to mention the female percussionist in the band, referencing her skills on both the tambourine and the triangle. He reminisces about the times he would sit on the triangle and hand his grandma the tambourine. As I listened to Mr. Withers speak so eloquently about his love for his grandmother, I was mesmerized by his choice of words, his tone and the musical phrasing, I felt so much internal joy and peace - so much love.

I still think of this as one of my very first conscious communions with God. It was the first time that I could honestly sense that although segregation in the South was still very bad, I knew that nourishment to the soul would often make its way to me through sounds and words of wisdom and a compassionate artist. I sensed that God was still creating miracles, and that there was light at the end of the tunnel. During these times I always thought of my great-grandma Peyton humming an old Negro Spiritual, "...da sun was gonn shine after a while".

Bill Whithers was one of the many great song-writer poets who seems to have been influenced by the Church.

In the late '60s Albert Ayler, a great jazz musician recorded a musical master piece: *Music is the Healing Force of the Universe.* Around that same time Dhyan Yogi, a great sage from Gujarat proclaimed that *Sound Vibration Nourishes the Soul.* Music is powerful and the Soul gets caught up in a state of rapture.

When I listen to music, the sound penetrates my soul, the vibration is like the *kundalini* rising; the coil or the corporeal energy, the unconscious life force that lies quiet at the base of the spine often activated by the energy or shakti and teachings of a great Yoga or meditation master. In my world, music is Yoga. Sound is often the vehicle that takes me to silence, and silence takes me to the deeper levels of meditation.

In Oklahoma, we had many medicine men and women who made up herbal concoctions for us. Traditional medicine always included the use of sage and sacred herbs, lemon, honey and whiskey, fasting, and prayers. The music was often chanted in unknown languages or spoken in tongue. When I was a kid, there was not a lot of talk about Sweat Lodges and Peyote Ceremonies, but we had some powerful healers. Someone was always making sounds and moaning ritual prayers to God.

Where I am from, the *spirit-warriors* were common community folks who made herbal concoctions, spent time in nature hugging and talking to the trees, and dancing in the bush with the animals, the birds, and the bees. *Spirit-warriors* are like the gurus, swamis, and Himalayan masters in the Yoga tradition who live to the rhythms of the earth, the sun, and the moon. They are healers, and at times they go into a trance and make primordial sounds. They speak in tongues (while in a super-natural state) - what some religious people call a language. Those sounds are often healing vibrations, they open your heart and allow light to flow into your soul.

I knew then that these prayers, and the singing and chanting by the *spirit-warriors* were a way to shift consciousness and go into the spirit world, like taking a simple walk in nature and listening to and observing the birds, the bees, the clouds, and the trees. All these rituals, songs, prayers and chants were life, and they were woven into everything that we did.

All these dimensions of my childhood propelled me on my journey towards what is now called an *Alternative Lifestyle*.

SEGREGATION

We were segregated, as per the time, but like everything else, that had two sides to it. We knew that being in the wrong place at the wrong time could be very dangerous and we knew that we were forced to endure terrible indignities.

Yet, the segregation caused us to live closely and lovingly. We had Grandma Peyton, Momma, mother and dad. We had all of mother's siblings and sometimes, if mother liked daddy's family, we had daddy's siblings. On top of that, all of the neighbors were nearby.

There were aunts and uncles, cousins, play sistas and brothers. We never felt alone, and we stuck together and tried not to go out in the evening. We lived in a big community. We were like a tribe.

My mother made sure that I did not go anywhere alone or, if I did, only to places that she knew were safe. She was adamant that we did not deviate from our routes. She did not want us to inadvertently expose ourselves to any possible unexpected harm.

When I was a child, I believed that my mother could fix anything. But when my little brother died suddenly, I saw that she could not bring him back to life, and that was a major ordeal for me. The death of my brother from natural causes, made me feel like my soul was drowning inside my body and the pain was so awful that I just wanted to take my heart out so that it could rest for a second, from the pain. I remember that day like it was yesterday. I did not fault my mother for not being able to fix my brother's death, but I began to understand that there were things beyond the realms of what was around me and in front of me, and I felt a need to understand these strange and incomprehensible truths and rhythms.

I have always loved song titles. Titles are phrases that often have a lot of potent energy, power and truth.

Listen to Strange Fruit. *Billie Holiday; "Jazz At The Philharmonic."*

Growing up in the United States Of America, I had a fear in my soul that lived inside me for a long time.

Natural death was incomprehensible to me, as was another kind of

DEATH

The Death caused by Segregation and Discrimination - it takes your breath away - and I knew it all too well.

We had our system, and they had theirs. We never crossed the line, but they crossed it from time to time and when they did, it was never good. Segregation and discrimination are friends to no one. They leave an imprint that does not easily dissipate. But music can soothe and heal the soul, and Yoga can give the soul a road map that takes you from darkness into light - if you allow it to.

The *Three Cousins*, as we called the KKK - the Ku Klux Klan, rode into our neighborhoods in the middle of the night looking for trouble. We had to hide underneath the table so that the KKK did not see us and set the house on fire. As we sat in fear I replayed gospel songs in my mind, and I thought about this land I so loved and drew strength from it, and from all the many people I loved around me. During those dark times, a path presented itself; I learned that *surrender* - a complete *surrender* to God - helped me to see the *light*. Through this *light* my fear was contained, and I kept following God's voice.

You see, our people never ventured into others' neighborhoods to commit violent acts of terror, and I hope that someday history will clearly record this fact. We were not the ones who covered our faces and rode into strange neighborhoods and committed genocide.

Because of the *three cousins*, we lived in fear, a fear that created tremendous faith in God within our community. At an organic level, my community had to adapt codes and principles to live by, that allowed us to keep our dignity and to stay pure in thought, word, and deed. I learned that it is very important to stay pure and focused, and to live the life that you believe in, even in the worst situations. Our own version of the Yamas and Niyamas became our protection. Of course, at the time we did not call our actions by those Sanskrit names, we just realized that our actions mattered.

My understanding of the Yamas and Niyamas are based on the many ancient texts that I have read over the last 40 years, the main book being Patanjali's Yoga Sutras and its many interpretations and explanations.

The Yamas and Niyamas are the first two limbs of Yoga's eight-fold path and they form the foundation of all Yogic thought and practices. Without practice of Yama and Niyama, no spiritual progress along the path can be made.

The Yamas

ahimsa - non-violence

satya - truthfulness

asteya - non-stealing and not taking that which is not given

brahmacarya - sexual responsibility and regarding others as humans and not as male and female bodies, and

aparigraha - abstention from greed.

The Niyamas

sauca - cleanliness, including internally in the form of avoidance of impurities such as anger and egoism and moderation in diet

santosa - contentment

tapas - austerity and commitment to our Yoga practice

svadhyaya - spiritual self-study, and

isvara pranidhana - surrendering oneself to God.

This code of behavior frees you to take ownership of your life and to direct it toward the fulfillment you seek. Some people call them Yoga's ethical practice. Although I didn't know it at the time, our response to the *three cousins* was to respond in a manner that upheld the principles of life, which kept strong our ethical values and beliefs.

Our experiences and our ethical beliefs were not hypothetical situations. Each one of us saw ethics and nonviolence prevail. Even as a small child, I knew that *Rosa Parks* stood up for what was right, and that it worked - it affected change. She carried the torch that ignited the flame. There are many accounts written about her and the bus boycott. *The Henry Ford Museum* provides an insight into her story through its online article, *"The story behind the Bus"*. What a lovely title!

On December 1, 1955, *Rosa Parks,* a Black seamstress and member of the *NAACP*, refused to give up her seat in the Black section of the bus to a White man. She was arrested and the Montgomery Black community began a bus boycott that lasted for 382 days. The boycott ended on December 21, 1956, when the Supreme Court ruled to de-segregate bus services. This incident launched the beginning of *Dr. Martin Luther King's* Civil Rights Movement - a nonviolent peace movement for social change. To this day, if I get on a public bus, I will not go to sit in the back. And, I did not go to the movies for a long time. Going to a movie theatre still brings up the memory of being a second-class citizen, sitting on scant metal chairs.

I experienced and learned a lot in Oklahoma. My childhood there was filled with so much of what I call *spirit energy*, and people who believed in and worked for peace and freedom. People like Grandma Peyton, the medicine men and women, the spirit warriors and healers strongly influenced me. Blacks in the US in the 1950s and 60s, were the *untouchables* and we had to learn to survive and flourish within our own culture and ways. We nourished each other through some of the most difficult times in the history of the United States.

The mystical spiritual energy of Oklahoma carried us through these times, we kept our voices through music, and by decoding the language and the lyrics to communicate with one another, so that those in the majority culture did not understand what we were saying. This energy nourished my whole family and gave Momma, my grandmother, the strength and energy to live to see a Black President when she was 100 years old, or 'thereabouts'. For both of us, Mr. Barack Obama as President was monumental.....is monumental. WOW! All the way from the back of the bus to the White House. Can I get an................................*AMEN!*

The racism, segregation, discrimination, and genocide did not go away. My experiences as a child in Oklahoma prepared me for the ugliness of racism and discrimination. These things sent me into a silence that came from fear, a fear that tore a hole in my heart and soul. Over time Yoga and music purified my soul and fixed me so that I could find peace. Music lifted my soul and my spirit, and Yoga acted as a guide for living my life.

WEST GERMANY

याभिषुं गिरिशन्त हस्ते बिभर्ष्यस्तवे ।
शिवां गिरित्र तां कुरु मा हिंसीः पुरुषं जगत् ॥

Yabhiśuṁ giriśanta haste bibharśyastave
śivamgiritra tām kuru ma himsihpurushamjagat

Mountain-dweller, mountain-guardian, make that arrow you hold
in your hand auspicious: do not hurt humanity or the world.
—Shvetashvatara Upanishad.

I often think about the years that we spent in West Germany, where I lived from third grade to junior high school. In Germany, there was not only the absence of people of color but also the absence of color - although it is a country filled with history and art, tragedy and war, there was not much color in the surroundings.

I cannot say that I loved Germany, and I'm not sure I even liked it for that matter. Knowing what I know now, I'd say that they were years that I spent inside - they were quiet years, and I was afraid most of the time. I went from the great plains of Oklahoma where my great-grandmother lived next door and Momma lived in the house with us, and all of the people on my little block were like me - colored and farmers. A place where I could lay in the grass and look past the tip of my nose and see forever. In Oklahoma, I knew everybody and everybody knew my family, in fact, everyone was family and we were so happy because there was so much love.

Germany was cold, dark and grey and the people did not smile much. In fact, they stared at us and called us 'schockoladen schwartze' or 'chocolate blacks'. Only a small minority of the residents on the base were non-White. Every once in a while, a German ran up to us to see if the color would rub off our skin, and then they would ask us to turn around to see if we had tails. At times, we felt as if we were on display; everything was so strange and really difficult because we were just kids and it made us feel awful. We often traveled in twos for safety. But after some time, we realized that the locals were just curious about us and maybe not truly racist. We were just as odd to them as they were to us.

Good and bad always happened on the base. The bad thing was that the *good ol' boys*, wherever they are, are the same. The first year that we lived in Germany I went to summer school. I caught the military bus to school each day. I was the only Black kid standing at the bus stop with the other students from various parts of the US.

One thing that my family taught us was how to act around White people. They didn't speak to me, so I didn't speak to them. One day, one of the boys said to me, "Where ya from?" I answered, "Fort Sill", knowing that giving the name of the military base would make more sense to him than saying that I was from Lawton. He looked down his nose at me "Yeah, thought you was gone say something like that, you sad-diddy Nigga!"

I just stared at him. In Oklahoma dogs were often used to attack Blacks and Native Americans. We were taught from the time that we were little kids to stand tall, set a fearless gaze on them, stare directly in their eyes, try to make contact with their soul, if we thought they were about to attack. So I stared at him that way, directly in the eyes. I did not blink and if looks could kill, he knew that he would be DEAD. On the bus I heard the kids in the back giggling and saying, "The uppity thang don't have to sit in the back of the bus here in Germany".

Little black children growing up in the US in the 50s were told never to cry, so I did not cry. We were taught how to deal with an over racist society;

don't cry, stand tall, speak loudly and clearly, avoid areas of isolation - there is safety in crowds - but growing up like that, in such heaviness can take a toll on even the brightest of souls. To be a child and not to be allowed to cry was tough. We were not allowed to be children. But I also did not feel that I had to separate myself from everything I knew - I *knew*, that I had to be present. I was in the second grade and I had to survive.

The day was gray. In fact, the rain started before the bus reached the school. I just wanted to run and lie in the grass and look at the tip of my nose and see forever. Instead, I felt like this country was another planet, and I was not at home. That day at school, after being called a *nigger* - the way he said it - I sat at my desk all day and heard nothing. I didn't even hear the bell ring at the end of the day. Before I realized it, I was at home with my sisters and I didn't want to talk about what happened. I just wanted to feel the safety and love that I feel when I am with my family. Even though we lived in a very strange place called Stein Castle - yes, a real spooky 14th century stone castle - we were together and that was what mattered; that made me feel good.

The next day, I was at the bus stop again, and four of them were giggling and pointing at me. As I walked towards the bus, the spokesperson for the group said: "So you half red and half Nigga? Well, well" he said, "you mighty lucky to be living here where you can go to a good school with us good Whites, you can go to the same toilet with us, eat in the lunchroom. My pa said we need to get you to help us out with our books and stuff to pay for the privilege of being here, so I thought I would just have you hold my book bag since I gets a little tired from the walk here. Here, take this," and he threw his bag to me. The bag fell on the ground and the books fell out. He screamed, "Pick up the books, Nigga". I didn't move. I stood and looked him in the eyes. I didn't move and the bus came by and stopped, and he told the bus driver that I tried to steal his bag. The driver was a local who, of course, spoke English very well and said, "I don't believe you. She is too small to steal your bag. You are a very big boy. She is afraid of you". His three friends burst into laughter and start calling him fat boy. Although I didn't like seeing anyone being bullied like that, I felt better because the bus driver stood up for me. From that day big boy's buddies engaged me in friendly conversations.

TACOMA - WASHINGTON

लोके 'पी भगवद्-गुण-श्रवण-कीर्तनात् ।

Loke'pi bhagavad-guna-shravana-kirtanāt.

> *The world devotion grows by singing and listening to*
> *Lord's praise. — Bhakti Sutra*

I was so happy that we were in our final year at the military base in Germany. I was excited about going home, being *stateside* again, and maybe seeing Momma and all my friends and neighbors in Oklahoma. I was imagining the sweet smell of green grass, listening to grasshoppers, and eating corn right out of the husk. Yes, I could taste the goodness of life again.

Then we got word that the KKK had struck big time. One of the organization's well-known members placed sticks of dynamite in a Black Baptist church in Alabama, where young children were attending Sunday school.

The blast killed four young Black children:

Denise McNair, age 11

Addie Mae Collins, age 14

Carole Robertson, age 14

Cynthia Wesley, age 14.

The verdict was *Not Guilty* of murder. The man responsible for this horrendous crime was fined a 1,000 dollars for possession of dynamite and six months in jail. Fear set in - that all too familiar feeling afraid everyday was back - and then, we learned that we were not going back home but to another military base within the US.

Our next stop was Tacoma, Washington. Even though I was not back home in Oklahoma, I was a teenager and could feel that life was about to get back on track. But, the day we left is imprinted forever in my mind, as it is in everyone's mind who lived through that day. It was the fateful day that the President of the United States was assassinated in Texas. I kept hearing people say that the commander, the chief, was shot. Maybe because we were kids, we were not told the full extent of the tragedy right away, so like good children we crossed our fingers all day and said little prayers to God that things would turn out all right. But somehow, deep in our souls, we knew that it wouldn't. That empty foreboding, that I always felt in Germany, kept creeping into my mind and somehow I just knew that things wouldn't be okay.

The assassination shook us up. We were *army brats*. In military school, we were told all about US might, US power and US right. And then, our own President was ... SHOT? I was convinced that nothing was safe, not even our White leaders.

We arrived in Tacoma - it was raining, it was cool and it was gray. This was going to be a major adjustment. Nowadays, what we experienced is called *"Processing and Re-entry"*, but back then it was just *returning to stateside*. New friends. New climate. New habits. And me, a teenager, a new person.

I was sent to junior high school in Tacoma, Washington. I wasn't crazy about classes, but I liked school and I found that I had a good voice, like my mother. My music teacher at the new school wanted so much for me to study opera. She rushed to tell me about each and every classical music opportunity that came to the school. I longed for that big, fat sound and the control that opera singers have, but one day, I passed a Pentecostal church and heard a voice that reached all the way out to the sidewalk.

I rushed in to see where it was coming from. A woman was standing in the front of the pulpit and her mouth was so wide open that you could see into her throat. She must have been about 5'5" tall, and weighed close to 220 pounds. Her arms were spread wide like wings, and her heart completely opened to let you jump into the rhythms and sounds coming from the very depth of her being.

When I reminisce on the experience today, I think I would have stood there and thought, *"Sarah Vaughan, Mahalia Jackson, Etta James, Little Shirley Caesar, Aretha Franklin, Gladys Knight, Jessye Norman...* all wrapped into one?" But at the time, I only knew the voice of Mahalia Jackson. When I think back to listening to Sister Pearl's voice, all I knew is that her voice defined the term *"rhythms of the world."* I surrendered then and there because I was mesmerized by her voice. I felt that I had been *born again.*

In church they often say "something got a hold on me" and in Eastern thought: "my *kundalini* was rising". Waves of joy instantly filled my heart. I wanted to join that choir and, lucky for me, my mother agreed to let me go to the church with the pastor's family, because they lived five minutes away, and had girls my age. They would also deliver me home after each rehearsal and service.

In a church community, there is always talk of those who are born with the *gift*. Well, Sister Pearl sure had the *gift* and shared it every Sunday.

I immediately joined the junior choir, which allowed me to see Sister Pearl every Tuesday, Thursday and then again on Sunday. She fascinated me: she was larger than life. When you see someone blessed with a talent that is almost transcendent, they become icons. I watched everything that she did. I took mental notes. What did she like? Who was she close to? What did she like to eat? Who were her friends? Why was she not married?

I quickly learned that she lived a simple life, a life of devotion to Pastor, Jesus and her family. She was a devout Christian and always referred to Jesus as *Sweet Jesus*. For many years, she worked as a librarian and after she retired, she spent hours at the church serving in whatever capacity she could. She and her brother took care of their parents, they lived in the same house, worshipped at the same house of God, and served in the same way she did. She was a very happy lady, always giving 100 percent and expecting the same from others.

In the choir, you had to crawl before you could walk, meaning you had to put in many hours of practice before you were full on with the mic. I liked Sister Pearl's rules because the discipline helped me build the confidence, patience, and humility that I needed to stand in front of a packed church and sing. She liked my voice. She said that I had a little of that boy-girl thing going on, a second alto, tenor drone-like voice. I really did not know what she meant but I was grateful because she actually noticed and listened to me sing.

Sister Pearl had her rules for the choir; speak softly, which was a hard one for me because my low deep voice, always drink room-temperature water, herbal tea, and warm honey water, constantly sing softly to yourself and do not sing if your throat hurts. Rehearsals were mandatory. Even if you could not participate, you had to be there.

We had other rules, but they did not put me off because I was a military child. I knew about discipline and its benefits. The Church even gave us more rules; we had to mentor one child from the children's choir; we were to maintain at least a B average in school and parents were expected to come to the performances held both at the church and in the community. Family members were accepted in place of absent parents, given the circumstances. All of these rules helped us feel like we were part of something wholesome, connected and about love.

Every other Sunday, we sang. It was exciting to sing with people, to really make sounds, and to lose oneself in the power of music. The choir had a set of cliques and as with many group dynamics, there are the *chosen ones* who get to lead. In the beginning, that was okay with me because I felt that I had a lot to learn and - like every other singer whom I have known - I was shy and always hide behind others.

Sister Pearl spoke often at the church. She told us that she did not feel that she had any special gift. She said she appreciated the compliments she received, but felt that her love for God was what actually got people to

29

listen and praise. Her belief was that all voices are good but it is truly the level of one's faith and devotion that hooks the soul into the groove, into the magic.

We knew that many talent scouts came to the church on Sunday mornings looking for that gifted singer sent by God. One day, we found out that Sister Pearl was offered a signed contract and we were all excited. But she told us that she turned it down because she did not want to sing secular music. She was a gospel singer. "I sing to my 'Sweet Jesus'. Praise the Lord, Hallelujah…"

Then she went into a trance, stood up and shouted, "I got up off of my knees!" and the choir members who were scattered throughout the congregation, stood up with the beat, and responded: "Hallelujah!"

Sister shouted it again, "I got up off of my knees!"

Choir: "Hallelujah!"

"I got up off of my knees!"

Choir: "Hallelujah!"

"I got up off of my knees!" Sister then said, "I said I wasn't gonn' tell nobody."

Choir: "NOBODY!"

"I said I wasn't gonn' tell….."

Choir: "NOBODY!"

Sister: "But then I ran and I told…"

Choir: "EVERYBODY!"

Sister: "Then I ran and I told….."

Choir: "EVERYBODY!"

This dialogue lasted for 45 minutes, maybe even an hour. It was like thunder and lightning and there was so much kinetic energy in the room. All I could do was be present; in the moment. People danced, shouted, and praised God's holy name.

This church environment was another prelude to my life as a yogi. I saw the energy go deep into the soul and saw it transform the mind. This healing energy that is generated by sound heals the universe, by connecting the dots, the body, mind and spirit unite and become one!

I like to think of Sister Pearl as the Mantra Guru with a different kind of mantra. She didn't chant Sanskrit mantras but her voice and singing had the same ability to purify and heal the soul. She could ignite the spiritual energy in the body, sending all in her presence into another world. This felt like the same energy that is sometimes activated through the use of sacred formulas of ancient mantras, these vibrations create mystical states of consciousness. At that age, I could not articulate the feelings that were aroused inside of me from the music that I listened to, either at church or at home. I could only feel the intensity of love and happiness that filled me when I listened. Sometimes music would simply *quiet* my senses or stabilize my mind and allow me to slip into elevated levels of consciousness and bliss. I did not understand these experiences then, but these are the places that my spirit traveled to when in the rapture of Sister Pearl's singing divinity.

Meanwhile I carried on like any other teenager. I was a *candy striper*. I played lots of sport, including gymnastics and volleyball, I ran on the track team and I danced. But my main passion was singing. I wanted to study more music but my mother just could not afford lessons, so I kept singing in the choir.

Anyone's teenage years are a strange blend of excitement and frustration. The body and mind both change. Sometimes these experiences are positive and sometimes they are just difficult. The body develops a new form and the mind starts to like as well as dislike changes. Girls start menstruating, *ladies' holiday*, as it's called in India, and the boys have wet dreams.

For a few years, we try to ignore it all, and then somehow we surrender to it and start to think that we are so clever. If parents are around, they try to keep you as a kid for as long as possible, not because they want you to remain a child, but really because they know what's about to happen to their dear sweet babies. The tug o' war begins and continues forever.

The ways of our parents and elders cannot be defeated, each generation has a job to do. Each generation enters a world already in motion, we are simply handed the torch and it is up to each of us to participate and do our part, whatever it might be and as confusing as it might sound, it is the only reality there is. We might fight with our elders, but the elders represent what is. But quiet as it is kept, there's no competition really, their wisdom versus our cool, it takes living and experiencing your life to actually see that there is no winning over wisdom!

I did the usual teenage things, but my somewhat eccentric side was already starting to develop. The conventional life was not attracting me at all. As a kid, I had many dreams about the universe and I always felt that we must have a sister planet that shared the same type of inhabitants as the earth and that I had a sister and brother from another planet who felt more of the realities and fantasies of my heart and soul. In my reality, there was no pain, suffering, or death. I just could not get my head around the idea of people being born only to die. I would actually obsess on this topic for hours at a time.

Several 'revolutions' were going on during my teenage years in the late 1960s. The spiritual energy was high, grass-roots organizations were everywhere; you could work for women's rights, civil rights, gay rights, environmental issues, there was an organization for every type of political and social issue that existed and people participated. You could be a hippy whose job was simply to give out flowers to people in *The Haight*. We were in the height of awareness and everyone wanted change for a better life. I was a hippy by choice and there were all kinds of illegal drugs everywhere, but my mother told us that we could die if we got high. One of her warnings was, "you'll lose control and lose the power of your mind." That frightened me more than anything. I did not want to experience altered states. I had no trouble imagining different realities by simply sitting without taking any drugs. Added to that, I did not like the smell of cigarettes and marijuana. Every one smoked it, had to have it and even I tried it. But marijuana did not make me feel anything other than sleepy and I wanted to spend my time working for peace and social change.

Although I did not partake in the drug culture at all, the hot political climate had a big effect on me. The Civil Rights Movement was in full force, and the activists for social change and justice were on the job day and night.

We Shall Overcome was the mantra for the times. To this day, Dr. King is one of the most important and influential figures in my life. My mother was my first guru, and then came the great MLK, **The Dreamer**. Through his *Bhakti*, his love for God, he ignited the spirits of millions of people throughout the country. He inspired them to seek to attain the seemingly unattainable.

Dr. King and his wife, Coretta Scott King, spent five weeks in India in 1959. After this visit, he was more convinced that **non-violenc**e and peaceful resistance were the way to true freedom. Dr. King used Mahatma Gandhi's teachings and methods of resistance to launch the Civil Rights Movement in the US. I think that his trip to India must have been a pilgrimage to the motherland of peace.

घरूद् घरूद्चरूरुरु इश्रूद्यछुप्रश्च रूभरुरू दृश्रूज्ञदाहरुरुदृश्रूज्ञचरू
चघरूट्ररुक्षरूषछुप्रश्च रूभत्रू

Yadvai van nabha vishyatnadharmo nadharma vyajnapa yishyat.

> *Without the power of speech, justice and injustice could
> not be known. -Chandogya Upanishad*

AUGUST 28, 1963

This date really stands out. It is the day that the Reverend Dr. Martin Luther King Jr. took center stage, stood on the platform at Washington Memorial and recited his famous **I Have A Dream** speech. Dr. King was joined by an estimated 250,000 peaceful protesters in the largest march ever held at the capital.

When I look back it was both real and surreal at the same time. Words are so powerful. I was real young when he gave that historic speech. I was almost a teenager; very open to the information that was floating around. I was trying to make sense out of life as I experienced it. I was always trying to understand the why's of racism and segregation. If you read the speech or listen to the dialogue, he covers each and every detail of the problem. I feel like it is a 'common sense' speech.

I love how he mentions the Constitution and the Declaration of Independence.

The March on Washington was the coming together of people - red, yellow, black, brown, white, all saying to the Government: "The Constitution is there. Deliver."

As I sat and listened to the speech, I cried at times. I smiled, I knew and I understood very well that the chains, the shackles of slavery had been replaced with the shameful, degrading, humiliating institutions of discrimination and segregation. One hundred years after the Emancipation Proclamation was signed - we were still considered second class citizens.

In my favorite of all Dr. Kings speeches, *Drum Major Instinct*, it reveals the heart and soul of the humble giant. He speaks about how he wants to be remembered. He talks about his love and devotion to God and family and the struggle for peace and freedom.

In my studies of all things Hindu over the past 40 plus years, Lord Ram enters my thoughts. Lord Ram incarnates to save the world. Hanuman is the devotee of Lord Ram. His humble servant, it has been written, that he is the "breath of Lord Ram." He is the symbol of selfless service, he has unconditional love for God, and total surrender.

Dr. Kings Bhakti, his Pure Love To God, his will to serve and be an *activist* for peace in the Civil Rights-Human Rights Movement, is a display of Pure Devotion and the essence of love. For me he is Guru.

If you look at the words in all of his speeches, better yet, listen to the recordings, you can hear the tones and the quarter tones. Listen to the delivery of the speech, listen to the musical phrasing and the dynamics of sound in his voice. At first there is a little space in your heart which slowly opens, and gets a little bigger with each breath. Before you know it, just the sound of his voice supported by your own soft gentle breathing takes you into the realm of *nirvana* and freedom rings, not only from the rooftops, but in your heart and soul.

I think about Dr. Martin Luther King Jr. daily. There was something in that style of preaching and teaching that opened my heart and made me choose to walk in the light.

The Civil Rights and Human Rights Movements dealt with the social ills that we were living with but no one took on the self-worth issues that so many of us felt. We were stripped of language, religion, culture. We were not allowed to relieve ourselves because of our color or eat food in restaurants because of our color. We were not allowed work to take care of our children or ourselves Because Of Our Color. So, too many of us started to become invisible to others and especially, invisible to ourselves.

A new voice came onto the scene - the voice of Stokely Carmichael; Kwame Turĕ and The Black Power movement. Turĕ urged Black pride and Black socio-economic independence.

Whenever I think about him, I hear Nina Simone's voice singing, *Young Gifted and Black*. Turĕ had a beautiful dream. At times, he spoke about integration and equality, but he also saw the need for us to take a look at ourselves and reconstruct our shattered and ruptured souls.

The message that I got from Turĕ was, *Let's stand up tall and proud*. When I look back now at Brother Kwame Turĕ, I think about the Negro spiritual, *My soul looks back in wonder at how I got over*, Mahalia Jackson, *In The Upper Room*, which was about prevailing when faced with obstacles and looking back in wonder at how one survived. Turĕ was an essential voice and leader in the Black community and will always be loved because of his willing spirit to work for social change. He spent many years in a self-imposed exile. It has been said that the time away softened his image and allowed not only himself, but his followers, to understand the need to comprehend the self, through knowledge, wisdom, and self-expression. I take his use of the word *revolution* to mean "let's change this world" to make it a better place for you and me.

Both these men were activists, philosophers and profound poets on the stage of life, at that time, giving us hope, igniting the flame, the Shakti. Dr. King spoke words in a way that made people really sit up and listen, that made people think he was a special kind of leader and I was amongst the millions who found it impossible not to tune into his message. His message was clear: have faith that tomorrow is going to be a better day; work toward the goals of equality, peace, and unity; be the truth that we talk about and believe, believe in idealism. As a people, we weren't just looking to integrate, we also wanted to stop living in a world of danger and wickedness as *less than*.

These freedom fighters spoke about a world I didn't know: one in which I wouldn't have to live with fear - the fear of not being able to ride public transportation, the fear of the KKK, the fear of being demeaned, ridiculed and prohibited.

I watched Dr. King on TV on the march from *Selma* into Montgomery, Alabama. I watched him go to jail in Atlanta for something as stupid as a *traffic ticket*. I watched him lead the March on Washington where it seemed like the whole of America finally stood up and demanded equality. Everybody was there - famous actors, musicians, politicians, church leaders, and people from every walk of life - like a giant ocean. Dr. King brought everyone together through the strength and power of his words, and his vision of a world in which people would be looked at for who they are.

So, on April 4, 1968, when Bobby Kennedy announced that King was gone, it made us feel like there was no tomorrow. For many people his assassination felt awful. It felt like war was being declared on the African-American Community, we were working for peace and justice

What happens now?

We stayed glued to the television. It was very much like the pain that so many of us felt during those horrible days of 9/11. People kept dropping by our house and we just stayed together, grieving. People slept over. We all moaned and groaned, and we cried loudly.

MUSIC HEALS

The moment I heard Mahalia Jackson soulful voice singing the words of *Precious Lord Take My Hand And Lead Me On,* I felt a shift. I felt the spirit coming from the four corners of the Earth and somehow I knew that for Dr. King and the Civil Rights-Human Rights movements, We Would **Overcome** this tragedy.

In the meantime, I had some overcoming to do at home. My mother wanted me to put my feet on the ground. She did not know what to do about her artistic daughter who had her own *dream,* who was looking for spiritual and political answers. She wanted me to settle down, think about life, maybe college or take a civil service job and go somewhere secure. But I had already decided that being secure for me wasn't going to come by following the status quo. Our family was getting ready to move to Hawaii, to another military base. Just before our departure, we were sitting in our kitchen and my mother looked at me very keenly, shook her head, and said, "I don't know what's up with you."

In Hawaii, we all began to see what was up with me.

DHARANA

देशबन्धश्चित्तस्य धारणा ।

Deśabandhaścitasya dhāraṇā.

Concentration is binding the mind to one place. —Yoga Sutra

Dharana is the concentration and focus that all of us need to get things accomplished in our family, in our community, and in the world. The place where I began developing my own Dharana was in Hawaii. Hawaii led on to California and from there, I was on my Yoga way. Hawaii was where I began to integrate the values of Yoga into my life - peace, spirituality, and doing work that improves the quality of life of those in need.

From my late teens to my mid-to-late twenties is when I experienced my own kind of un-interrupted Dharana. I began to understand what I needed to do to jump-start my journey.

The manifestations began to appear on a military base, in the farmlands of Hawaii on the Island of Oahu. I was a teenager still, in 11th and 12th grades, a true hippy girl walking barefoot and wearing long skirts with a big Afro. I liked people and I still had my 'practice' of music. I was popular at school, danced, sang with a rock band, sang devotional chants with friends, and wanted to live deeply and freely. I didn't care what my artistic form was, I just wanted to live in that peaceful place of the soul.

My high school was near the pineapple fields, where a community of Yogis were living. I admired their gentleness and their concentration. There were marijuana growers in the mountains who were truly leading a laid-back peaceful, open life.

At that time, I had a *sort of boyfriend* or whatever that means when you are 16. Jarue was my best friend, and still is. These days we rarely see each other, we rarely talk, but we are connected and our lives continue to intersect.

In Hawaii, we developed a total fantasy world. He lived off the army base in a small town called Wahiawa, where we all went to school. His father had a farm and he built Jarue a small cottage on the land to make him feel comfortable because his mother, whom we considered at the time to be strange, left him and his father one day and never returned. Jarue's father was always trying to compensate for the lack of a mom by giving Jarue lots of freedom. To me, he had an enviable life, because we're a tight-knit, strict, military family and my siblings and I had to fight for every ounce of freedom.

Jarue missed his mother for a long time, but he told me once that his father was such a good dad, such a strong role model, that his mother's departure did not hurt so much anymore. He would've welcomed her back of course, if she ever wanted to return. We spent a lot of time talking about our feelings, our views on life, the hot political climate, and who we saw as the leaders of today, yesterday, and tomorrow. We had dreams about a new world in which none of the *isms* would exist, a world in which we would not be judged by our skin, and we tried to develop character that was strong and true to what we knew to be truth at the time. It all felt so full of hope and promise.

A military base can be a friendly place. One day, Officer Pete, who lived next door said to me: "Here, I have this book. I think you'll like it."

The book had been given to him by one of the young military recruits stationed there. I felt that Officer Pete was subliminally saying: "I've got a weird book on my hands and you are the right combination of weird that might get something good out of this book."

I said, "Thanks" and he handed me the book.

He told me that he had glanced through it and the poses looked interesting, and some of the text pertaining to life was also interesting.

"Enjoy it," he added, "and let me know if it ever comes in handy."

He didn't know it, but I was extremely touched that he understood that I was not just a wacky 16-year old. I thought that he too might understand that we should all work together to *Change This World And Make It A Better Place To Live.*

I didn't know at the time that Officer Pete's book was a gift from the universe that started me on my journey. The title of the book was *"The Yoga System of Health and Relief from Tension"*. It was a very basic book with simple instructions and beautiful black and white photos. I love that book and, after over 40 years of Yoga practice, I still refer to it. In fact, it is my Yoga Bible. His gift was an honor.

It turned out that there were a few Yoga classes taught by a Mr. Kumar at the base chapel. Some hippy kids like me attended, as well as some military wives. I didn't know much about the rules of life, but I knew enough to know that if you choose a path, any path, and follow it, you end up somewhere. So I decided to choose Yoga. At that time, I didn't really understand it or why I chose it. Mr. Kumar did some breathing exercises at the beginning and end of each class and I felt something happening, and it felt good. He taught simple standing poses, simple sitting poses and breathing exercises. Breathing was very important and we spent most of the class working on the breath. He ended the class with Savasana.

योगश्चित्तवृत्तिनिरोधः ।

Yogaścitavṛtinirodhaḥ.

Yoga is stopping mental activity. —Yoga Sutra

I could see that Mr. Kumar was teaching us to be centered. The Yoga Sutras defines Yoga as "*the cessation of the fluctuation of the mind.*" It took a while for me to understand that I needed time and work to get the mind to focus on a single thought, and that the journey is not so easy because it brings up both joy and pain. Mr. Kumar always started with a scripture, a philosophic or spiritual statement, or even something current going on in the world. Then, we did sun salutation and his guided meditations.

Mr. Kumar also gave me a book, *The Yoga Sutras of the Great Sage Patanjali.* The Yoga Sutras are considered by many to be the authoritative text on Yoga, and were compiled around 2,000 years ago. I loved this book too. At the time I did not know of any Black churches with magnificent choirs in Hawaii, so Yoga replaced that connection for me. Yoga fulfilled my need to go deep into the world of the unknown and to commune with God. It also provided me with a deep, meaningful counter-culture comfort zone to exist in, to learn in and to grow in. It represented exactly what I was looking for.

I started practicing Yoga and Jarue joined me. But since he was a year older, he moved away to go to the University of California when I was in the 12th grade. In many ways, he had become my inner voice or, maybe, my spirit was somehow set free through him and I started to voice my feelings in a way that was foreign to me and out of my comfort zone. But I also took this as a sign of the times, when we all got up and expressed ourselves. We were at that time in a *hippy, free love, be thy self* frame of mind. We had the music of Motown, Rock, Jazz, and the early 70s bought us **The Messenger** - the great Gill Scott-Heron.

Jarue stayed in touch by hand written letters and occasional phone calls, even from California, and we kept up our dialogue about life and what we were looking for. He was a habitual marijuana smoker, and even did a few hits of acid now and then, but he was trying to stop his daily smoking. He told me a story about meeting these guys who were doing a very different type of Yoga practice. He kept mentioning it and said that the classes were not far from his dorm. He sent me one of the posters which said something about altering states without marijuana or acid. Both of his roommates had tried the classes and they nagged him to come along for the ride, he found the situation very funny because although the guys in his dorm did not stop smoking pot right away they slowly changed some aspects of their characters. They became vegetarians and their actions softened, they seemed to be more responsible and were very peaceful.

So Jarue thought he would try it. Just one visit and was hooked on the man with the turban. *Yogi Bhajan* was his name and *Kundalini Yoga* was his path. The path of the *kriyas* - cleansing techniques, *pranayama* - breathing techniques, and devotion, these teachings changed Jarue's life forever.

Jarue and I spent hours on the phone and writing letters to each other about the depth of the feelings that we were experiencing from participating in the 3, 7 and 21 minute kundalini exercises. *Yogi Bhajan* taught a series of cleansing exercises called *kriyas*, which were very rigorous movements synchronized with controlled breathing sounds, breath retention, and accessing the *Mula Bandha*, allowing us to feel lightness physically and spiritually.

The bond between us, as well as my desire to remain a part of Jarue's life, was the initial motivation to learn all that I could about this sacred path of kundalini. I became very focused on breathing, sound, and silence. Through Jarue 1 was introduced to Yogi Bhajan's style of pranayama, kriyas, and devotion. Eventually, Jarue got a real girlfriend, a sweet young Kundalini Yoga devotee, and our love moved onto another level.

Meanwhile, I graduated from high school. I also moved on romantically and met Tyrone from New York City who was cool, wore beautiful clothes, and had superb taste. He was not a hippy-surfer boy, like most of the guys in Hawaii. In fact, he hipped me to the fact that there really were not that many Black hippies and definitely not many Black hippy-surfers like Jarue.

My new boyfriend and I had a very different type of friendship that involved physical intimacy, which was not something that Jarue and I had, at least not at the physical level. Jarue was like my brother, my best friend, and - at times - my teacher. I thought I was madly in love with Tyrone and, to make a long story short, I eventually got pregnant six months before he was discharged from the military and married him. Once discharged from the military, he left for New York and never returned. He left me but I had my beautiful daughter, and I got a divorce.

Jarue and I stayed in touch through all of this and we shared a fantasy that one day we would be together. Jarue wanted me to come to California, attend the university and feel the vibration of the time. He wanted me to taste the essence of the *peace and love* movement to see the many grass-roots organizations working for change that was so much a part of life at that time. He wanted me to see and be right in the thick of *I'm Black and Proud!* movement and spend a day giving out flowers in *Haight-Ashbury*. It made sense to me. I was too young to get a good job and didn't know how to do anything anyway. So why not college and a new life?

At that time I wasn't feeling safe in Hawaii. My close friend Biggin was into growing weed, as a lot of kids were then. I was with him one day and I caught sight of some guns, and it scared me enough to exit the friendship. I decided to go to San Diego. I immediately enrolled in San Diego City College and then on to San Diego State to study Counseling and Correctional Education. I sent my daughter to Oklahoma to live with Momma and Auntie, where I knew a little girl could have the best childhood that a child could have.

Before I left Hawaii, the Kumars shared with me some of their thought and beliefs. I remember Ms. Kumar saying that if I incorporated and lived by the rules of Yoga, my life would be a happy one. To date, I feel this was the best advice that I have ever received. Whenever I spent time with them, I listened eagerly to them talk about the philosophy of Yoga and living in harmony with God and nature.

They always made reference to observing silence and the importance of just being still. I saw through their lives how natural and beautiful life could be and, through the weekly meditations, I experienced deep levels of silence that I soon learned were a direct passage to God. So when Ms. Kumar suggested that I incorporate and live by the rules of Yoga, it made sense. Early on I thought that she was a bit wacky. But by the time I left Hawaii I had developed a tremendous respect for her and the life that she had chosen. My heart yearned to do something very similar. She sent me on my way with the gift of a beautiful simple meditation which is a part of my day to day life:

"Give silence at least one minute for each hour in the day."

In the early years of my fledgling practice, I sat two times a day, for 12 minutes each time, in the early morning and then at sunset. Now, both my morning and evening sitting is for 24 minutes. I get to a beautiful place simply by listening to the sound of my breath. That's all.

I placed my daughter in the loving arms of my big family in Oklahoma, and I caught the bus to San Diego where I lived for the next ten years. I was not alone; I lived with my auntie, my cousin brother - her son, and my oldest sister, who by this time had lived in California for about two years. But that was the problem. I was from a large family and I had lived with family all my life. Now I wanted to be with myself, quietly, listening and developing.

I was so happy, loved attending university, studying and meeting like-minded people. We all had big afro hairdos and we wore peasant skirts and when we wore shoes, they were the Chinese cotton shoes, so that we weren't killing animals for the leather. One part of me was a vegetarian and meditating hippie and the other part was an activist, fiercely committed to human rights and I loved all the grass roots community organizations like

SNCC (Student Nonviolent Coordinating Committee) movement for social change; one of the organizations of the Civil Rights movement.

At university and at work I met a lot of people of color. There was also a lot of holistic living going on: fasting, Yoga, whole foods and everything related to a healthy hippy lifestyle. I got a job in a hip juice bar near my apartment and met everyone in the hippie world. In the meantime, I kept investigating more Yogic disciplines; *Hare Krishna, Kundalini Yoga, Shiva-nanda Yoga, and others.* As Momma would say, *"Life will learn you"*, translated: *"Live and Learn"*. That's what I was doing.

Jarue came to San Diego and spent time at the juice bar where I worked; he faded in and out of my life. He lived in Humboldt County, a big hippy area that was so hippy-centric that people smoked marijuana on the street without fear of repercussion. By this time, Jarue had done a tremendous amount of introspective work on himself, and Yoga was his daily therapeutic practice. We both went to therapy with Running Cloud, my powerful native-American therapist, who had a long ponytail and the energy and wisdom in his eyes that my grandfather had. Although I was the one booking the appointments, Jarue came along because he also needed some under-standing and clarity.

I went to classes, worked, and practiced basic *Hatha Yoga.* I was an assistant teacher for several Yoga classes and spent a lot of time in meditation. The classes grounded me because I felt unfocused, my behavior and general attitude were typical of young students of the time and I was probably too open to everything and everyone.

I hadn't become part of any center, system or path since I had not yet found *My* Teacher. I talked to various Indian Spiritual teachers during their tours in the US. I was extremely inquisitive, asking "Why does God let us suffer so much?", "What about genocide?", "Why are people starving?" It took me a while to learn that these great teachers don't answer questions. They guide you to the door way of silence and the answers come from going into silence. At times I also sensed that some teachers had prejudices towards gay people or those who had chosen paths of life and religions different from their own. I finally understood that teachers and Gurus, are humans with human failings. I learned who to spend time with and who to say thanks to and no thanks to. For me, it was about inclusion not exclusion.

I lived in San Diego for ten years and became part of the community. A lot of those years were in school. And, of course, there were romances and even marriages. My second husband was Ricardo, a kind, good person, and I thought I needed this because I was all over the place back then. I had lots of interesting relationships. But Ricardo was a sweet man, perhaps a bit too laid back for me, and I was getting deep into politics and community activism and not really set up to be a Miss Stay-at-Home. We parted as friends.

I directed my focus back into Yoga and meditation, chanting Sanskrit mantras while being quite confused over the revolutionary fervor of the time. I embraced the movement for social change, and I felt my job was to be part of social organizations that were working to improve the community. I started volunteering at various community service centers.

I was still at school when I met a handsome academic provost at the university who was 20 years older than me. Carlo had a seductive New York accent. We sat on the beach and talked and talked. He was one of those men who knew a lot about a lot of different disciplines and I was enthralled, listening and learning. Carlo was my real education. He spent some time preparing to be a Catholic monk in his life, which of course he did not become, but it gave him his academic backbone and knowledge. He was fluent in many languages and could speak about many topics. He also knew and fully understood the practice of silence. It had been a part of his monastic life. He taught me how to listen, which opened me up to learning. I soon learned the importance of receiving and observing information.

My daughter came to live with us and it was a lovely time for me. We traveled together in a van through Mexico and Central America and I learned first-hand about those cultures. Carlo loved art and taught me a lot about paintings and Italian and European culture and its music, especially that of Italy. I was constantly being introduced to new facts and ideas. Of course, we had our ups and downs and the relationship wasn't perfect but he provided me with a home and the quiet and safety to grow.

Carlo was Sicilian - he was never really sure if he was White or Black. But he opened my mind to the huge umbrella of discrimination. He was not White Anglo- Saxon Protestant. Once I was with him while he was teaching a class at the university and because of his Italian name and ethnic looks, one of the kids said, "Maybe you'll teach us how to gamble and how to place that winning bet." He said that he receives negative feedback like this regularly. I came to realize that Blacks were not the only group of people who were stereotyped and misunderstood.

Around this time, one of my Yoga teachers advised me to do *seva* ; the Sanskrit word meaning service, to always be available for those in need and to be aware that service is an opportunity.

So I began to volunteer with several grass-roots community service centers. I wanted to work in any capacity with anyone who wanted to work for human and civil rights. In San Diego there were people volunteering from all walks of life—from construction workers to doctors and lawyers, to bakers, teachers, carpenters, babysitters, and hairdressers. We set up shelters and worked wherever there was a need. We provided food and set up soup kitchens. We tried to do whatever we could to help those in need in community shelters and halfway houses.

The Black and Latino establishments in San Diego donated food, clothing and a variety of services. As a neighborhood community center we provided breakfast programs, counseling, child care, and after school educational programs. We really did not know what we were doing half the time but we knew that we wanted to help.

One of the most controversial grass-roots community service organizations of the times was, *The Black Panther Party for Social Change and Justice.* A lot has been said about them. The aspect that I became familiar with was the spirit of community, sharing-and-caring for each other. It was truly inspiring and uplifting, their expressed love for community and justice made it easy to get focused on working for change - the flame called 'hope' - was red hot. The energy or Shakti that so many community-based programs imparted was and is still very important in urban communities.

When we were growing up in *America*, we were excluded from all things *American* and the Community organizations helped change that. The goal of Community Based Organizations is inclusion. The communities wanted to be included and simply wanted their story to be told. The communities wanted to be in the history books, in schools, in the teaching profession, on TV, and in the movies… in every aspect of life in the United States, even pop culture. The community people want to be acknowledged. African-Americans are not immigrants, we came on slave ships and worked hard to make this country a country. The grass-roots community based programs for social change and justice for all were simply movements against racism and discrimination. The philosophical platform was to instill dignity and to restore a future in challenged and at-risk urban communities. At times it was obvious that some of the community leaders' methods were very different from Dr. King's but make no mistake, he was the 'Leader' and the goal for peace and freedom was the same.

The general platform that the Community Centers for Social Change presented and implemented were incredible. They ran after-school programs/daycare, tutoring programs, medical clinics in the community, food co-ops, and job counseling and placement, just to name a few. With the help of many outside groups and agencies, and private funders, their work slowly began to make a difference in the communities. Lives were changed and people went to college and returned to work in these same communities, inspired to become self-reliant. Public schools today still have programs that provide free day-care, and after-school care, that serve free breakfast and lunch, regular nutritious meals having been proven to enhance learning. These programs were initiated by many of the grass-roots movement, for social change in the spirit of loving children and wanting to end racism and discrimination.

Many of the key members of the grass-root organizations knew that social economics play a big part in the reality of *how we roll*; who we are and what we believe in. The social change movements worked to educate and support freedom and peace, beliefs at their core, and their work was based on the principle that all people should be treated with respect - a human right.

We all Must Do Something to stop Racism and Discrimination.

So I threw myself into it. I participated in many early morning breakfast programs on the south side of San Diego. We'd pick a spot in the community and serve breakfast to the neighborhood kids. We were grass-roots so there were times that we would run out of food but we felt we were fulfilling a basic need - we were feeding hungry children. Eventually these programs received funding from community church organizations and private benefactors as well as a variety of funding agencies and organizations. It was fun to be with other community workers like myself. Sometimes we brought in organic food from organic farmers outside San Diego as we wanted the kids to be healthy. The centers that I worked in also provided free check-ups for women, and provided contraception if it was wanted or needed. We informed immigrant women in need of care, about the free clinics available to them.

One of the favorite things I did at the Center for Social Change was the evening Yoga program. At that time, San Diego was a Mecca for holistic healing, health food restaurants, health food stores, and Yoga and meditation. You could find Yoga and meditation classes each and every day and people considered it important. At our Center, we did lots of Hatha Yoga classes with basic sun salutations simple meditation. We practiced kundalini breathing and Jarue often came to town and led the class. Many of the members at the center where I volunteered, felt that Yoga was an important part of building a strong body and peace of mind to weather discrimination, and the courage to change. People whom I knew in the community and in the various movements felt that Yoga was a wonderful guide for living a healthy wholesome life, and was just as important as eating organic health food.

तपःस्वाध्यायेश्वरप्रणिधानानि क्रियायोग: ।

Tapaḥsvādhyāyeśvarapraṇidhānāni kriyāyogaḥ.

> *Yoga is a discipline for purifying the body, breath, and mind by physical, mental, and spiritual service. – Yoga Sutra II.1*

During these years, I began to piece together what the Yoga Sutras and yoga meant for me. I saw the practice as disciplined action, a study of the self, and surrender to God I saw yoga as that life that we live and those things that we do. I started to understand living yoga "off the mat."

यमनियमासनप्राणायामप्रत्याहारधारणाध्यानसमाधयोऽष्टावङ्गानि ।

Yamaniyamāsanaprāṇāyāmapratyāhāradhāraṇādhyānasamādhayo'ṣṭāvaṅgāni.

> *The eight limbs of yoga are outer restraints, inner restraints, seat, breath control, sense control, concentration, meditation, and absorption. –Yoga Sutra II.29*

Yoga has *eight* limbs, which are simple and good principles for living life. Whether you are working for Civil Rights and social justice or in community-based service programs that are enhancing and enriching life, these principles give us a solid foundation.

1. Yamas - ethics

2. Niyamas - conduct

3. Asana - yoga postures

4. Pranayama - breathing techniques

5. Pratyahara - controlling the senses

6. Dharana - concentration of the mind

7. Dhyana - meditation

8. Samadhi - absorption in the infinite

Ahiṁsāsatyāsteyabrahmacaryāparigrahā yamāḥ.
Jātideśakālasamayānavacchinnāḥ sārvabhaumā mahāvratam.

अहिंसासत्यास्तेयब्रह्मचर्यापरिग्रहा यमाः।
जातिदेशकालसमयानवच्छिन्नाः सार्वभौमा महाव्रतम्।

> *The outer restraints are non-violence, truth, not stealing, chastity, and not coveting. These restraints form a great vow that is universal and not abrogated by birth, place, time, or circumstance.*
>
> *—Yoga Sutra II.30 & 31*

The foundation of yoga is made up of the same ethics as those of Mahatma Gandhi, *Dr. Martin Luther King Jr.,* of *Jesus Christ,* and of the *Buddha.* A common thread running through their teachings is: We are all one and we share the same rules of love, life and nature. What we have in common as people is more important and useful than what makes us uniquely different and special. When we come to the table we are all God's children. We are all the same red, yellow, black, brown or white; we are sisters and brothers. God is our father and the Great Earth is our Mother.

San Diego woke me up to some amazing realities. I saw people living in communes sharing everything and caring about each other, the planet, the animals and the environment.

I remember admiring the beautiful California sunsets, knowing that the gas and fumes floating around added a dimension to its beauty - it was very psychedelic and I realized the all-important need to clean that up. The rules of life have no borders and no barriers of language, race, or creed. I loved what I saw in California; so many folks trying to work together as one. This was how I wanted to live and I wanted to move my spirit and mind in line with this thinking. I felt drawn, I felt that I was being called and I knew that my work would be to weave yoga into every aspect of my own life as well as the lives of others.

I knew that it was really time to go to work. I became a Yoga teacher, practitioner and a life time student. Before the onslaught of today's Yoga popularity explosion and Yoga studio boom - this was still a time when Yoga was truly a spiritual practice and not so much about being a way to shape the body. **Now, of course, Yoga absorbs all people regardless of their intentions.**

After ten years in San Diego, Carlo and I relocated to Boston for his work and I anticipated what life would bring there.

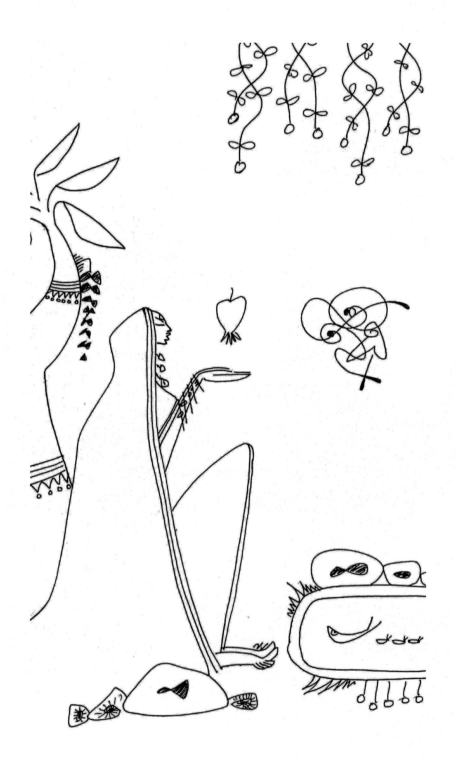

PRATYAHARA

स्वविषयासम्प्रयोगे चित्तस्य स्वरूपानुकार इवेन्द्रियाणां प्रत्याहारः।
ततः परमा वश्यतेन्द्रियाणाम् ।

Svaviṣayāsamprayoge citasya svarūpānukāra ivendriyāṇāṁ pratyāhāraḥ.
Tataḥ paramā vaśyatendriyāṇām.

Sense control occurs when the senses imitate the mind in meditation

by not attaching to their objects. This results in ultimate mastery

of the senses. —Yoga Sutra II. 54 & 55

P ratyahara is taking control of the senses and living the life you are meant to live, the life that comes from your center. You get there by listening to your inner voice and being willing to serve. If you do that, you will end up on the right path.

Carlo and I moved to Harvard Square in Cambridge. I liked the small town and the university environment, and the seasons reminded me of Oklahoma. Boston still had a strong hippy community in the 1980s. Harvard Square was made up of students, academics, and people "doing their own thing", be it running architectural firms, *Bead and Head shops* or record and book stores. Boston was a walking city - people promenade through the Commons, through Harvard Yard - just like New York, and that was beautiful. The Charles River was near the square and spring, summer, fall or winter, one could walk by the water and sense the quaint New England beauty, big trees, a calm in the air and history.

Carlo made friends with some MIT peers and it didn't take me long to see that they all may have had rocket scientist minds but financing themselves on marijuana. In fact, when I looked closely, most of the alternative businesses in Cambridge were financed not from street traffic coming into the shops to buy, but from marijuana. At that time, the marijuana business was the oil business of the counter culture.

Carlo missed California so he went back and forth, back and forth, and I began to get used to being on my own. As I did that, I could see that my days as his 'student' were coming to an end. I was ready to be an adult - my own person. I told him that I wanted a divorce. We thought that we would grow old together, but we realized that the age gap was edging us apart. At the time, I slowly started to live my own truth and moved away from his.

I moved to Back Bay, an area of brick row houses that looks a lot like *Edith Wharton Country* or nineteenth century England. The Back Bay was also a great walking area with its cobblestone sidewalks, big maples and weeping willows. One felt the solidity there. I began doing odd jobs, secretarial, whatever, but I soon realized that what I really wanted to do was teach Yoga seriously.

I began teaching a little here and there, at the Cambridge Adult Center in Harvard Square, the Boston Adult Center on Commonwealth Avenue, other community centers, shelters that my friends ran, and halfway houses. The community program that I worked with was facilitated by the courts, which assigned former inmates to halfway houses. One of these programs had several houses scattered throughout various neighborhoods in Boston, Dorchester, and Roxbury. I was contracted to work as long as there was funding, but the money always ran out and about half of my classes were volunteer work.

Everywhere that I taught, the people responded. I found myself moving all over the Boston area and to Roxbury and Dorchester, and developing a strong community of friends and people who were busy serving the community. These same people led me to places where I taught Yoga as a kind of social work because it truly healed people who were going through traumatic events, such as homelessness or just getting out of prison. Yoga helped them to calm their anxiety and gain a stronger sense of who they were, and gave them the tools to face their challenges. In addition, any strengthening of the body strengthened their self-esteem and increased their ability able to move forward into healthier opportunities. I taught classes at Harvard University in one of the many student activity programs and spent several years teaching Yoga for the American Repertory Theatre at Radcliffe College in Cambridge, Massachusetts. Many of these actors found me when I moved to New York and joined my classes while working in the theater in the city.

The majority of my work was in half-way houses or innovative experimental programs working with women in crisis. Most of the programs were sponsored by community service operations and government agencies and the clients, where still under the jurisdiction of the courts. I worked very closely with their probation and parole officers and a tremendous amount of my time was spent in rehab centers.

The theme was always restructuring, refocusing and starting over. Most of the women were second and third-generation drug users who had babies and were struggling with themselves or the system, or both. Many of them, however, had been sober for a long time and were working hard to get their children back. For some reason the weekends were always hard.

On weekdays the schedule for both the women and the kids was full, with every hour taken up with therapists, psychiatrists, medical appointments and job interviews and of course, school. Weekends was allotted as time for the participants and their children to have quality time together without too much intervention. Although this was invaluable time, sometimes, it was challenging because a large percentage of the participants had no parenting skills, as well as no patience, so I was eventually asked to come on Saturdays or Sundays to teach Yoga and breathing exercises, sometimes even including moms, and kid's Yoga class. That was a lot of fun and the noticeable changes showed up right away. Mommy and child seemed less anxious and by the end of class everyone, myself included, felt relaxed and sported big smiles straight from the heart.

It was a tough environment, a lot of the young women would go out in the evening to party a little and be very angry the next day. The halfway houses had a large turnover of residents, but they were excellent programs with strong track records of success and helped a lot of women get their lives together.

Most of the programs offered Yoga classes and meditation sessions three or four times a week and, because one thing leads to another, nutrition classes just happened. I wasn't a trained nutritionist, but I shared with the women what I knew about healthy eating. They constantly teased me and told me that I was square, but I think that I served as an inspiration because I seemed different from them. Many of my activities were unfamiliar to them. Meditation and yoga were a daily part of my life, I ate healthy food, fasted and attended silent retreats, I used no make-up and as an alternative to leather I wore cotton shoes. For these women to abstain from meat was a big thing because the only time they did this was when they were broke. I also didn't go to night clubs with them and didn't drink alcohol.

We talked about the alternatives to fried chicken, barbeque wings, and pork chops, and because we had use of a big, beautiful, fully stocked kitchen, we cooked some good gourmet vegetarian *soul food*. We started a herb garden and before long, the pots in the kitchen were filled with collard greens, mustard greens, cornbread, baked sweet potatoes, and mashed potatoes with gravy. We made all of the dishes that everyone was familiar with but without meat and *fat back*.

We had so much fun growing the herbs and preparing the meals and many of the women were interested in healthy eating. Some even became vegetarian.

I learned so much from these women, especially those in difficult situations. Sheree was a resident in the program and became one of my Yoga and group therapy students. She was serving time in a community, post-prison halfway house that I was assigned to. Three times a week my colleagues and I facilitated group and individual therapy, Yoga, meditation, eastern philosophy, and devotional singing.

Sheree spent many years incarcerated. She entered the system, in her early 20s and I met her, in her 40s. Her two children lived with her in the halfway house, and as far as I knew, they basically grew up there. They were possibly the very first guests in the house. Sheree was considered a very positive inmate at the halfway house and therefore she was given privileges. Her education exceeded mine and most of the others who worked in the program. She had two doctorates and a post doctorate, and was the senior counselor for the program and taught in the *GED* and *SAT* programs at the facility.

Sheree spent a lot of time reading and doing research for other women at the house on their own individual cases, and she spent a lot of time advising them. She was a true jailhouse lawyer. She also worked out a lot and became interested in cooking because she had decided to become a vegetarian.

She loved discussions about Eastern philosophy, the many Indian languages, Indian food, and the fact that a large percentage of the country was vegetarian. She loved talking about the Indian economy and how poverty in India had almost a different flavor than poverty in America. She felt that the history of poverty in India and America had very different beginnings. Therefore they both had their own brand of discrimination.

We had great discussions that often made us laugh and cry and think. One day we had a crazy conversation about *bleaching cream* and which country in the world sold the most bleaching cream, at the time we could not Google it, but someone said that according to a Black magazine in America, Africa was number one and a close second was India.

Indians come in many differing shades, and I have seen many very black, beautiful Indians. The old-school institutions of racism in America and caste in India are still works in progress...

Sheree knew about my travels to India and the importance I placed on my Yoga and meditation practice. She knew how much I loved the country, and we had fun talking about India and the US. I expressed to her the gratitude I felt for Mahatma Gandhi's vision and philosophy on non-violence and peace, since it is one of the philosophies that inspired Dr. King's Civil Rights Movement. It was the umbrella for social change. Dr.

King and Mahatma Gandhi both represented how ethics, principles, love, devotion and commitment can bring change. We had this great discussion one day that the 8 limbs of yoga represented the tree of life. The Civil Rights/Human Rights Movements are about the human experience being inclusive as well as living in honor and with dignity… this is Yoga.

I learned so much from Sheree, an amazing God-loving woman. She had a magnificent presence and the ability to transform the energy in any room she walked into. When I first started working with her, she made jokes about Yoga and playfully acted as though she did not know much about it. But the program's participants were given three weeks notice before we started and she, of course, spent that time reading about the path of a yogi. She read the *Autobiography of a Yogi* and knew about the current mystics from the East currently being talked about in certain circles in the US.

We had many discussions about service; the honor of being a parent and doing selfless work, to be a school teacher or a nurse or a man on the street who collects garbage, or the *lower caste* who drives a rickshaw to be able to care for his family. We talked a lot about the love that we both felt for people like Mother Teresa and for the unknown volunteers who live all over the world. We constantly spoke about what it is to do selfless service. And what it is to incorporate Yoga into daily life, off the mat.

अनिर्वचनियंप्रेम-स्वरूपं ।

Anirvachaniyamprema-svarupam.

The power of love exceeds all thought. -Bhakti Sutra

Sheree spoke a lot about *time* and I think about those conversations even now. She declared that time is God, something that I've heard others say since then. Of course, we constantly debated the concept of *time* and what it is, what is the black hole, did God create time, is time separate from God or is everything an illusion? Is time Freudian? Is it spiritual? Is it both? Or are they the same or are they different?

Sheree concluded that it is all the same, that so much is reliant on the mind and the perceptions; how we interpret information, how we process the information and what we can achieve through *silence*.

I remember those days well because we all looked forward to spending time with Sheree. She was like our Guru with her own groove. She opened our minds to understanding that all things are not as they look like and seem. She taught us to give every little thing a chance, regardless of how small it might seem.

For example, the family next door had two teenage boys who wanted to be gardeners. They asked if they could take care of the yard and grow a small flower garden, and due to their efforts, we had fresh flowers daily in the spring and summer. She reminded the women to thank the two young men for the gifts of roses and lilies and whenever the women made food and baked cookies or pies, the boys were invited inside and enjoyed the treats.

Sheree always said, "I'm serving time, I'm in time and on time. This is time and time can be beautiful because time can serve you." The way she said this reminded me of one of Momma's sayings, "it's not that bad. Just that way." A translation of this can be, "just accept it." Sheree accepted her life and made the best of it, and she taught us to do the same. I always felt as though when we asked her something, she'd go into another zone.

One day, I asked her to talk about her personal life and her two girls. With a big smile on her face she recounted: "The only thing that I have been attached to since entering this life is my girls. It was hard when they were not with me and in foster care. Then I heard that my dope addict sister was getting out of *rehab*. She was my only hope for the girls so I asked her to come to see me. I begged her to get my children. My dope addicted mother asked me if I was crazy! I said no. My mother said to me, 'What do you think? You asking her is like you asking me to take care of them.' I looked at Momma and said, 'No Momma, she is a dope head but she is family and she knows the truth.' Momma said, 'what truth you talking about girl?' I looked at my Momma right in the eye and I said, 'Momma, she knows about God's love.' My sister came in here and I saw and felt her peace, her love, her light. When I saw her I knew and understood her when she said, *I am walking in the Light and the Grace of God.* I said, 'Momma some things words cannot explain, but I felt better knowing that my girls were with her rather than someone who is a complete stranger to them who just want the monthly check and the food stamps."

Sheree continued, "There were times when it felt impossible but when you let God into your life all things are possible. It was a hard thing to set up but my sister hung in there, followed all the steps, the rules, got custody and then brought them to see me every time we could have visitors. I worked hard, followed all the rules, and did everything I could until I made it to the community house. From there I could start to petition for them to live here in the house with me (one of those new innovative programs). My girls both went to college - one is a social worker, the other one is a nurse. The two girls now work with women like me who need a little help from family and friends. My Momma in her own way was a good Momma, she did the best she could, given her knowledge of what she knew to be right for the moment and she gave me my sister, a great sister who found her way after drugs, alcohol, and jail. If it wasn't for her, where would my girls have gone? I wasn't there, I reached out not knowing if anyone would hear my voice, understand my pain, and answer my prayer. My prayers were answered."

The women in the program really struggled, had a lot of pain and went through great trials to rebuild their lives. Getting close to them was inspiring but extremely intense; thank God for Yoga and meditation! I eventually hit my *burn-out* point.

As much as I loved the house and the women, I needed a shift in the type of work I was doing. I had a connection with a wonderful group of Black women who were program writers for community-based centers that resulted in social change, and I asked them to find me a new placement. This next assignment was a beautiful senior citizens home. I was pleased, and it felt like a break! The seniors were wonderful to be with and their wisdom and joy just flow from their souls. I taught chair Yoga with the older people, using a chair as a prop to help them in the postures. They didn't exercise much, but seeing their enjoyment of movement, as limited as it was at times, was beautiful to see.

At that time, a senior citizens home for Blacks and Hispanics was unusual, but today they are gaining popularity and acceptance. All the residents participated in the sessions, the women looked over at the men and the men looked over at the women. We did chair exercises so that whole body could be supported and practiced walking meditation - eyes open, one step at a time. The seniors were great, it made me realize that with age comes a sense of peace and freedom.

ॐ भूर्भुवः स्वः	Om Bhuur-Bhuvah Svah
तत्सवितुर्वरेण्यं ।	Tat-Savitur-Varennyam,
भर्गो देवस्य धीमहि	Bhargo Devasya Dhiimahi
धियो यो नः प्रचोदयात् ॥	Dhiyo Yo Nah Pracodayaat.

OM Let us think on the ray of the rising sun, the first and best
of day OM. OM Let it illumine us OM. – Gayatri Mantra

One of my joys as a teacher was to integrate devotional music into my Yoga classes. This became my trademark. Mr. Kumar's teaching style was to read a little philosophy for us to meditate on. I chanted soulful Sanskrit verses, which eventually became recordings for practicing Yoga and meditation.

Sanskrit verses are so beautiful... as large as my passion was to sing Motown and Gospel music, I was also enchanted by the rhythm of Sanskrit words. I learned as many verses as I could and started singing them chanting them and absolutely relishing their sound. I speak English but chant Sanskrit verses sometimes not even knowing what they mean I just knew in my heart that they were beautiful phrases to God.

Sanskrit verses nourish the soul in the same way that I feel nourished after listening to or singing along with *Shirley Caesar, Mahalia Jackson, or Etta James*. I learned the chants, found a traditional interpretation, and then revamped and restructured them to my ear. As with anything that is done with love, people responded. In the Yoga classes at the high school we used musical phrasing that the students were familiar with, we used tambourines and triangles. Often the music teacher would send along students; sometimes we would get a bass player, a guitar player or even a trumpeter or a violinist - the goal was to elevate the spirit through sound.

Even today, when I teach Yoga at a high school in New York, we take the chants and turn them into rhythms that are funky and familiar, yet always show honor and respect to the lineage, or the tradition from which the chants came. The students were excited by the chanting and are transported to their center.

In Boston I experienced a variety of meditation techniques, I began deepening my Yoga practice and study. I researched extensively; Yoga history, Yoga philosophy and Yoga laws. I had a strong love for the 8-limb path of Ashtanga Yoga and the teachings of Sri K. Pattabhi Jois.

This method of Yoga involves synchronizing the breath with a progressive series of postures, a process that produces intense internal heat and a profuse, purifying sweat that detoxifies muscles and organs. The result is improved circulation, a light and strong body, and a calm meditative mind. The *Ashtanga* method eventually leads one to the full realization.

The rules of Ashtanga are almost monastic. Students should rise early for meditation followed by their asana practice. Preferably between 3 and 4 am. This discipline alone will change a person's life. Three am is such a beautiful quiet soft time of day. This intense quiet alone with meditation and prayer and a rigorous Yoga practice will restructure your life. How you eat, how you work and how you play, these things all change.

As your practice deepens you learn to integrate your family obligations into and around your practice. One of the most beautiful things about Ashtanga yoga is that the main vehicle for teaching is observation of the breath and an unwritten celebration of silence. Although it's a very disciplined path it is not difficult because it feels so good.

THE HOSPICE

Meanwhile, Yoga guided me to continue to work with people who were in need. As a counselor working in community service centers, I often had clients who were referred to *12-step programs* for a number of reasons. A woman named Naomi ran one of the programs, she was an ex-nun and a registered nurse. She suggested that I work with her at a hospice for HIV and AIDS patients, so I volunteered there as a Yoga therapist. For almost three years, I practiced in the morning and then volunteered at the hospice. I worked with people suffering from HIV and AIDS - I should really say, with dying people because being diagnosed with HIV in the early days was a death sentence.

The center was located in one of the small communities in Boston, in an area that I have always considered the 'hospital zone', right on the Boston Brookline Jamaica Plain line, in a beautiful historic Boston home that had been completely refurbished and made into a care facility for those suffering from this very scary disease. In the early years of HIV and AIDS, beds were scarce, so the hospice was a frenetically busy place. Patients were admitted and at times, within just a few short hours *Home Goin'* or transition into the other world took place.

At the hospice, I wore a lot of hats. Some days, I arrived and several emergency situations were occurring simultaneously. On those days, I was often sent to wait in the lobby, only to be told to go home after an hour or two. My job varied from day to day. One day, I might support a patient in a walker or guide a person who had lost their sight. I often chanted *AUM* or *Hallelujah* as we slowly moved up and down the hall, stopping to sit and catch our breath. Sometimes I simply helped patients to rotate their legs as they lay on their back. At times, we just observed the breath, "listening to the breath, hear the inhale, hear and feel the exhale." We used the breath to connect the body, mind, and spirit, and through pranayama, we often went deep into silence and meditation. There were also days on which we watched whatever was on TV.

इरूभरूश्र तमठ्इबरूभद्ध क्षज्ञरूत्तरूम रूक्ररूद्यरूज्ञरूएरूद्यरूक्ष

Tatahksiyateprakasa-avaranam.

> *Pranayama can remove what blocks the light.* —*Yoga Sutra II.52*

I usually went to the hospice two or three times a week. Sometimes, a patient and I looked at magazine articles and listened to the radio and I can still hear *Sylvester* singing:

> *Do Ya Wanna Funk*
> "Won't you tell me now
> If you wanna funk
> Let me show you how
> Do you wanna funk with me."

The patients came and went, some with families and some completely alone and afraid. Some asked me to call a relative just to let them know that they were in the hospital and that they were terribly sorry that their card had played out this way. At times I saw a lot of anger mixed with the fear, but fear became life, and life seemed shortened, taken away. They were all so different.

One day, I walked into a room to serve a patient a glass of water at his request. He asked me to sit down, asked me if I were afraid of him and of being in this place. He wanted to know if I thought that he was bad because he had the virus. He wanted to know if I would call his mother and tell her that he wanted to come home and die, he did not want to die in this hospital. He said, "I just want to see her again, would you please call her and tell her that I am not bad." He started to cry, we held hands and he just closed his eyes. I was not sure if he passed away then or later but I know that he was not there the next day. I called his mother and she came, and I told her that her son was a good person. Using another patient's words, I said that "his card just played out this way." In the early days of the virus, no one knew what to do. We were all afraid.

I'll never forget *Anthony*. He lived at the center for almost two weeks, longer than most patients. I'd walk into Anthony's room and he'd say,

"Hey Miss Yoga Lady. We gonna do dog pose up and dog pose down. Let's do some Surya Namaskara, salute the sun, and Namaste. Come on and let's get to it. I have had my afternoon shave, had my shower, I am feeling good and looking good.

He held a mirror in his hand and smiled as he said, "Look at that fine young man in this mirror." He screamed out loud, "Do you hear me and I know I smell good, I look good, I is a pretty young thang, let the church say Amen to that."

Then he'd say, "Come on over here and give me a big fat hug and let's get started."

Anthony and I sat on the floor on small mats that the center provided for us. We sat, in lotus pose, close our eyes, bring our hands together in a prayer position, and slowly start to chant 'Aum', holding it for as long as we could. Then we chanted 'Aum' again. We took long, deep breaths and then chanted 'Aum' again. We continued to chant 'Aum' and 20 minutes went by and all we heard was 'Aum' and the sound of the breath. I sensed that a very calm, quiet energy came into the room and before long Anthony extended his legs forward and lay on his back. I placed the palm of his hands near his navel center. His eyes remained closed and a soft smile appeared on his face and he rested. I placed a cover over him and I quietly left the room.

Just then I ran into Naomi. She was making her rounds as usual and she looked at me, smiling.

"My dear", she said, "share your joy."

I told her about the session with Anthony. I mentioned that we actually did sun salutes, Surya Namaskara. During the first sun salute, we did not hop back and forth but Anthony was strong enough and he stepped back and forth. I was amazed at his energy. In all the time that I had been going to the hospice, I had not experienced sessions with anyone that was even close to what Anthony and I were doing. I was so happy but Naomi very quietly reminded me that this is a hospice and, "even though Anthony has some real good days, he has a lot of complications that he is dealing with, so keep him in prayer, keep him in your heart."

She said to me, "I know that you adore him and that is beautiful, that is what he needs more than anything else at the moment, a little tenderness, a whole lot of love." I think she sensed the fact that I actually believed he would survive.

I felt so good after seeing Anthony. I returned on Thursday and we had a marvelous session. We practiced Surya Namaskara-A four times and one Surya Namaskara-B. We sat and chanted Aum, and we listened to Aretha Franklin. He wanted to listen to *Mary Don't You Weep*. I still remember the piano playing and the smoothness of the choir and Anthony getting up off of his mat and saying, "Let's march like the choir does when they are marching in for 11 o'clock service. Girl, it's Sunday morning and we are in Church, come on girl just follow me. Act like you, Aretha, and I will be James Cleveland when the bass comes in. Listen. Let it move your shoulders, allow your body to relax, and just feel the spirit." It took me back to Sister Pearl. I felt like I was in Church or in a temple and all of a sudden, the movements were synchronized, the breath was rhythmical. Body, mind, and spirit became one. We were doing Yoga at the hospice, Anthony became the teacher and I was his student. It was so beautiful, so organic.

On Tuesday I returned to the hospice, and immediately felt a heaviness as I walked in. I stopped at the front desk and asked, "How are things today?"

The receptionist said, "Well maybe today your schedule will change."

That was not uncommon in a hospice, but there was something in the way she said it. She looked up at me and said that Anthony was having a difficult time.

"There are two nurses in the room and his doctor is on the way and his pastor has been called."

My heart sank into that familiar hole that I knew so well. I could not let myself cry so I started walking toward his room. I knocked on the door and then poked my head in.

I heard a soft, weak voice say, "Come on in, Ms. Yoga."

I started walking towards the bed and for the first time I could see the lesions on Anthony. I could feel his pain. The nurse told me that I would need to put on a face mask and gloves to come into the room.

I said, 'No.' Anthony said "Yes! Come use the robe please but I want to hold your hand so please hold my hand." I held his hand and we sat. I heard a sound. It was Anthony, he was chanting 'Hallelujah'. I started to chant 'hallelujah'…... The nurses joined in:

"Hallelujah, hallelujah, hallelujah, hallelujah"

We chanted for about 15 minutes. We were all at peace and, with a smile on his face, Anthony completed his journey leaving this world. I felt like he had transitioned in praise. I felt his light. I felt his truth. I felt his love.

Thanks to God and Science there is medicine to *battle* what I still call *the scary disease.*

Aum shanti aum

I have seen Yoga truly assist people who are in transit from this world to the other world and it also helped with the sadness and the heartbreak that comes with losing those close to us to pain and suffering.

Music, Yoga and Meditation - my recipe for restoring the soul. I went to many jazz and blues concerts following my years in the hospice, it took a long time for me to say that it was painful work. I needed the balance of the music to lift my soul from the painful experience.

I went to see the great *Pharaoh Sanders* in concert. It was where I met my next husband, Alden, a jazz musician, and a Boston blue-blood living a hippy life. We had so much in common and our mutual values of being vegetarian and living with a social consciousness, and our mutual love of music kept us together. He had two adopted children from a previous marriage, and he was raising them as a single parent. Together we adopted another child, a baby girl baby. My daughter was almost an adult and we all worked on this family together for the next 11 years. One of his adopted sons had special needs and required daily therapy. Having a difficult child can deeply strain a marriage and tear a family apart. We couldn't settle into an even, natural rhythm but instead, were constantly dealing with the out-of-control emotions of the child. Everyone was on high alert. Alden and I eventually had to split because our lifestyles had also became too different; I had my rigorous Ashtanga Yoga practice and he had his music and art.

Ashtanga was my daily discipline, I eventually had the honor of meeting Guruji in early 90s at a workshop in New York City. Prior to that I studied with his son in California. When I met Guruji, he was sitting on the floor on the opposite side of the room, talking to students. Suddenly, he stood up and began walking in my direction. He came right over to me and in a very soft-spoken Indo-English voice said, "You practice with my son, Manju. How is he? He is a good son. Is he teaching you?" I said "yes" and he smiled that big, beautiful smile that he is known for, and it lit up my heart.

गुरुर्ब्रह्मा गुरुर्विष्णुर्गुरुर्देवो महेश्वरः ।
गुरुरेव परं ब्रह्म तस्मै श्रीगुरवे नमः ॥

Gurur-Brahmā Gurur-Viṣṇur-
Gururdevo Maheshvarah,
Gururveva Param Brahma Tasmai
Shrii-Gurave Namah.

I was ready to go to Mysore, a small city in south India where Guruji lived and taught Yoga. I was ready to study at his *Yoga shala*.

I went deeper into my Ashtanga practice and began taking three-month sabbaticals to go to India to study with Guruji. He passed on invaluable knowledge about the essence of Yoga and its inner workings. He spoke about honoring the lineage of Ashtanga Yoga and often mentioned the Sage Patanjali and the Yoga Sutras. Guruji believed in teaching exactly the way that his Guru had trained him. He taught six days a week and encouraged us to practice six days a week. His answer to most questions was practice. Ashtanga Yoga will teach you the art of living righteously. Do your part, commit with devotion and experience the love. Each posture synchronized with the breath will take you higher and closer to the goal of *Realization.*

Ashtanga yoga is hard work. Sometimes it feels good and sometimes ....*OUCH*, would truly resonate!

It is not a quick-fix, it takes patience, time, endurance. But if one stays with the rhythm, dedicates oneself to ongoing practice.....magic!

As a student of Ashtanga Yoga I learned patience and balance. The Ashtanga practice is very structured and leaves and internal imprint that allows one to unfold from the inside. Guruji, suggested that I move to an Ashtanga community. There were only two of them at that time, one in New York City and the other of course, in Mysore, India. I wanted to be close to my kids, who were still young, so I chose the US. New York was going to be my next stop, one that took me even deeper into the practice of Yoga – on and off the mat.

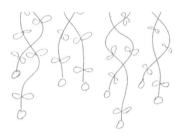

PRANA

यो ह वै ज्येष्ठं च श्रेष्ठं च वेद
ज्येष्ठश्च ह वै श्रेष्ठश्च भवति प्राणो वाव ज्येष्ठश्च श्रेष्ठश्च ।।

Yo ha vaijyestham cha srestham cha veda,
jyesthascha ha vaisresthas cha bhavati:
prano vavajyesthas cha sresthas cha.

Someone knows what is first and best, someone becomes first and best:
prana indeed is first and best. —Chandogya Upanishad

I have always wanted to live in New York City. That exciting city - the city of ambition - is where life challenges everything that you thought you knew. New York adds and strips you of foolishness. It will push you forward - if you are ready to go.

In New York, people can *reinvent the self* over and over. New York has a way of pushing a person and allowing a person to become the best that they can be. It is nourishing and competitive at times but one can *learn how to learn, by* sharing your discipline through dialogue.

New York is home to many artists, business and highly skilled people from all walks of life, so much passion and so much to learn.

After my divorce from Alden, I moved to New York City, Greenwich Village. In the beginning, I commuted back and forth to Boston to be near my daughter as she was still very young. During my early days in New York, I spent half the week in Boston. On top of that, I spent four months out of the year in Mysore. I traveled a lot, but I also felt settled and grounded because of my Guru and my practice.

The Light was ON. The New York Yoga scene had a very different flavor from the Boston Yoga scene. I felt that Boston had more of a community feel, people would post notices in Harvard Square and on the many community boards. I knew the community activists in Boston, which made Boston easy for my work. New York was an entirely different story.

I could not afford the high rents for a studio space and did not want to for that matter. I did not want Yoga to become a business for me. Yoga was my spiritual practice, my nectar, and my joy, and I did not want to change that. Many of my students were in need of affordable classes. I believe that Yoga should be for everyone.

I realized that one of the lessons that I learnt in India was that the masters and ordinary teachers alike all taught in in-house *shalas*. They taught at home. How wonderful. I loved the small group thing and I love the atmosphere of the Yoga Shala and I loved being at home. My life ended up being two batches of students, one at 5:30 am and then again at 8:00am, then off to teach at the High School at 2:00 pm, then meditation at 6:30pm.

On Sunday mornings since May 2000, my students from the High School, as well as the students from the early morning classes, would often join me for the 11:00am Puja at the Ganesh Temple in Queens. *Sri Maha Vallabha Ganapati Devasthanam* is a beautiful South Indian Stone and Granite Temple with exquisite carvings that depict the Hindu Pantheon. The temple was our weekly outing where we observed the Brahmin priest perform rituals and recite prayers from ancient Hindu text. The temple is a true community center providing classes in Yoga, meditation, Ayurveda, Vedic, Astrology, Sanskrit, Kannada and Tamil languages. Scholars from India come and offer workshops on the Vedas, The Upanishads and the *Bhagavad Gita*. There are also classes in classical Indian music and dance. *The Temple* is known for its dedication to Lord Ganesh and supports the American Hindu Community by honoring cultural and religious traditions of India.

Sundays were always full days at the temple. We prayed to God, we feasted on delicacies from the temple canteen and we prayed and chanted to the Lord again. It is such a beautiful celebration. India comes to you. The temple is fully equipped with a function hall and yes it hosts many traditional Indian weddings.

So to me New York meant:

Teaching

Chanting and the Temple

An excellent life

For me, one of the most important parts of Yoga, is sound vibration. Many have said that Mantric Sound and the breath will connect the soul to God. In the practice of Yoga all movement is determined by the breath, it is the key that opens the heart and the soul. Observing the breath creates an internal atmosphere that allows us to go deep into silence. That silence will bring us to Realization where we can commune with God. Chanting God's name continuously produces heat in the body. The heat increases and jump-starts the process of cleansing and purifying the body. Subsequently you start to feel joyous. You start to know that life is love and happiness. In the practice of Yoga, Guruji was able to manifest the same awareness by teaching in silence.

Chanting has always been an important part of my classes and more and more students kept asking me, to record my chants. Finally, after more than 10 years of saying that I would, I did:

- In 2000, I recorded my first CD, **Sacred Sounds Vol 1**, produced by the great jazz-violinist Mr. Charles Burnham.

- In 2002, I recorded **High Places** with the great jazz guitarist, Mr. James 'Blood' Ulmer

- Then in 2005, **Asatoma** produced by R/B drummer Leo Ferraro

- In 2007 **Puja** produced by Muthu Kumar

- 2009 **Tandava** produced by Srinivas Prasad

- 2010 **Unplugged** produced by Srinivas Prasad and

- In 2013 **Lord Ram** with Bill Henry, the musician whom I have played with for over twenty years. He is a gifted Jazz, funk, gospel, R/B pianist and organ player. He is also a Yogi.

My music is Devotional R/B, honoring the heritage of both India and the voice of Black America. For many years I played devotional music in Yoga *shalas*.

I have been incredibly blessed to work with gifted musicians and have performed in major cities in the US, Australia, Bali and India. My music is available all over the world. Courtesy of *CD Baby* and *TuneCore*.

An unusual opportunity for teaching yoga to inner-city public school children found me when I lived in Boston. I received a call from a man who said that he wanted to fund a yoga program for disadvantage at risk children living in Boston. He had a brush with ill health and became very interested in preventive health care. He saw the value in yoga meditation and healthy nutritious food, and wanted to start by introducing yoga to children at an early age. This was before yoga made it to the main stream so although he wanted to fund the program himself we had to convince the schools that it was beneficial. Eventually we found one school in Dorchester, one in Roxbury and one in Jamaica Plain, MA. The program was great and at the end of our seventh year my personal life changed and I moved to New York, where he was willing to underwrite the same gift there.

We offered the free Yoga program to many schools but none were interested. Finally, I found a charter school in lower Manhattan who said yes. There I had my first encounter with the *Crips* and *Bloods*. I worked with this high school for over 15 years. Even though I live in India at times I still go back and teach Yoga classes for the first semester of the school year.

Each year on my return the principal updates me on the changes that have taken place in the school. It is an urban inner-city school, and the student population is primarily Black and Hispanic. The teaching staff and administration is Black, Brown, and White, equally male and female, and class sizes are small. They call it a *last chance school*, where you must *get yourself together*. The students are very smart, some too smart for their own good and they all have fascinating stories and complex lives.

The Yoga class fulfills curriculum requirements for either Health or Physical Education, since we easily cover both. It is a co-op school one week they take class and one week they go to a work site. I think that is pretty hip, reminds me of North Eastern University in Boston, which has a very successful co-op program. I do not think of these students in the Academy as troubled inner-city youth. I celebrate them, viewing them as the poets and leaders of tomorrow.

Each young generation makes its contribution, has its specific themes, its ideals. Sometimes I have understood what they are saying, most of the time I just listen and pick out the things that are familiar. At times it seems as though we are miles apart but something will be said and something will happen that indicates that *We Are One*, and the game of life just has a new name.

I hear the bell ring. Seventh period ends. There is a break and I rush into the math room where I have been assigned to teach Yoga to the girls this year. Yoga always starts a few days into the semester, today is the first day.

I do a quick clean of the room moving the chairs sweeping and mopping the floor so that we can line the mats neatly before the students make their way to the room. They are noisy, laughing, chewing gum. I stand at the door asking everyone to remove their shoes and place them neatly under the counter.

"Why We Gotta Take Our Shoes Off", asks one of the young ladies. Another answers, "Cause this is Yoga and we are going to sit on the mats that are on the floor."

I quickly add that once the weather is warmer we will also remove the socks. **"Oh No That Requires Some Work, Ms.** You have to let us know in advance so we can get a pedicure or something cause the feet ain't right."

"Okay let's do this as quickly as possible, shoes off!... and please we need to get rid of the gum. Wrap it first, then put it in the trash by the door. Let's do this as quickly as possible. We need to get a solid hour of practice in. Come on ladies."

Finally we sit down. "Please let's have silence, first let's sign in. Please print and sign your first and last name. This is very important, it's the only way that I can really confirm that you are here.

"Okay my list has 14 names. This sign in sheet has only 12 signatures on it and I am counting 14 students in the room, who did not sign in. I need two more signatures on this sheet....." There's a knock on the door and another student comes in, "Ms, you the yoga teacher? They told me to come here."

"Why are you late?"

"Cause I was with the counselor and I need a PE credit so I am here."

"Okay take your shoes off and come in."

"What! Take my shoes off?"

A student yells from the back, "Just take the shoes off so we can get started."

She removes her shoes and then I ask her to remove and wrap the gum and dispose of it in the trash.

"Okay Ms, but I am not sure about this class. This is weird to me."

The late student signs the sheet and the two missing signatures are there.....we're good to go.

"Okay, next I am going to hand out writing pads. Please write your names on the top."

"Ms, I don't have a pen."

"Does anyone else need a pen? And does everyone have a pad? Do we need any more pads? Okay, this writing pad is for you to keep. Now I am going to ask you a series of questions and I want you to write both the question and the answer in the pad....."

"Ms, I thought this was a Yoga class. I don't want to write."

"Please write all the questions and answers in your writing pad. When you finish, close the pad and observe silence until the others finish."

There is some chatter in the room but for the most part everyone is participating, answering the questions I have given them.

"Okay, now all the note pads are closed thank you. My name is Ms French, Ms Regina or Sistashree, so you have some choices."

From day one, I am always referred to as Ms, or Ms Yoga Teacher, so I included some more names, but they somehow always came back to calling me Ms and that is okay with me.

"Now let's go around the room and each of you tell me a little bit about yourself. What your interests are. A little about your family life. Also, what you know about Yoga and why you have either signed up for this class or were assigned to this class."

To my surprise seven of the students in this particular group had taken at least one class in Yoga. One student raised her hand and said that she started yoga when she was a student at the uptown "John V. Lindsay W C Academy (our sister school)", she said she loved it. She has a baby and found that after giving birth the yoga poses and stretching were good for her body.

One student answers that Yoga relieves stress, stretches the body and helps to relax her. Another student felt that her experience with *Bikram Yoga*, helped her with her weight over the summer. Another student said that it keeps the body strong. Another response was that Yoga is for the body mind and spirit, then another response......breathing, stretching.

One student said that she watches Yoga on TV and still another student received a free one month membership to a posh Yoga studio in Soho.

As much as I have criticized the role of Yoga within contemporary popular culture, listening to the students makes me realize that it comes with benefits. Twelve years earlier when I taught the first Yoga class in this school, I asked the same question: "What is Yoga?" The response was, "Is it yogurt", "is it voodoo, what is it?" And many of the students wanted to switch classes rather than take their shoes off .....

We continue with a wonderful discussion about what Yoga is. I show them the books that we will use in the class. "Light On Yoga" by B.K.S. Iyengar, the other is "Yoga: The Iyengar Way" by the Metha's and an Ashtanga Yoga booklet by Richard Freeman and of course the "Yoga Mala" by Sri K. Pattabhi Jois, a text that is mostly beyond their level of understanding, but an interesting read nevertheless.

They look through the material, look at the pictures and ask a lot of questions. I notice that the time is running out so I ask the students to take note of the rules. Please come to class on time. Use the restroom prior to class. No shoes in class, and so on. This is a class, I say, about growth, being present, uplifting the spirit, nourishing, toning and being conscious about the body and embracing the soul. We will learn simple breathing techniques that can help us sleep, can promote energy and can change your perspective almost immediately. We are going to practice Yoga on the mat but we are also going to see if we can incorporate this into our daily lives *off the mat*.

I tell them, "I like to think of yoga as a big tree with many limbs. Each limb represents an aspect of who we are, our life as it is, and all the possibilities. So, as we climb this tree of life we become like the tree, grounded and rooted in the earth and we reach for the sky. All things become possible. Each class will start with the traditional Sanskrit invocation to the Ancient Sage Patanjali. This we will learn in class, then we will do a combination of yoga poses, starting with the sun salutations; Surya Namaskara A, Surya Namaskar B and the more advanced Surya Namaskar C. Then a series of standing poses which will include some standing breathing exercises, some sitting poses, followed by back bends, shoulder stands, headstands, breathing exercises and finally meditation, observing silence for 10 to 12 minutes."

Although there is a lot of structure to the class, I will be open to students working on poses that they find in books and are interested to try. There is a final exam, where you are expected to do the sun salutations A, B and advanced C, and to answer a few questions about the history and philosophy of Yoga.

I explain that we are here to work hard and have fun. We are responsible for removing the chairs and bringing them back in the room. I hear the bell ring.

"Okay it is time to go. Please help with the chairs."

They of course jump up and head straight for the door to sign out and get their cell phones and one or two of the students bring the chairs back into the room.

As I start to gather the books and mats to return to the shelves I realize that it really is a new day, and at some level *Yoga has arrived.*

At the next class I explain to them that the fourth limb of Yoga, according to Pantanjali, in the Yoga Sutras is the Yoga of the breath.

"Over many years of study," I tell them, "it has been found that the use of very basic simple breathing techniques have been used to treat a large number of stress-related disorders. It has also been found that people who practice the controlled breathing of Pranayama, develop strong minds, strong will power, and use sound judgment. It is truly the Yoga of awareness. I think that through awareness it becomes easy to *give peace a chance* and to *love thy neighbor*. Pranayama is the marriage of the individual soul to the universal soul.

B R E A T H E!!!

"Okay! So maybe I am getting a bit carried away! But try it….."

They laugh but are willing to go along with me.

"Inhale deeply, exhale slowly, listen for the sound of the breath. Just do it for three minutes it will change your perspective. So when out on the picket lines, the protests, breathe, *Yes We Can*, and remember to exhale."

The task of my generation was to connect into the future. Yoga provided us with the tools for the internal journey. So that we could Journey To the One, *Journey Towards God.*

And at times Yoga was for me Like a Bridge Over Troubled Water, it guided me over turbulent times.

I tell them that Asana practice and Pranayama are the two limbs from the eight that we will focus on at the academy. They are interested, proving how the soul yearns for connection. I feel their enthusiasm and openness to learn about the interior world.

Once school is over, it is quiet in the hall, the students are gone. I walk down the hallway saying good night to the teachers who are still there, quietly reviewing their day and it starts to feel like a Yoga shala where minds are learning how to think and walk in the light.

And I feel a happiness of imparting what is good, what can give and open, one to the other.

INDIA

ततः परमा वश्यतेन्द्रियाणाम् ।

Tataḥ paramā vaśyatendriyāṇām.

Drawing of the senses.

From Pratyahara, supreme mastery of the senses.

Tatahparamavasyataindriyanam. —*Yoga Sutra II.55*

The magic of India did not come upon me immediately. On my first trip I went to a beautiful *ashram* in the north with a large group of devotees from the US and Europe. Members from the ashram picked us up in a chartered bus and took us directly there.

We did all our studies and took all our meals in the ashram. They kept us under close watch. I was a little frightened to see the extreme poverty that India is renowned for, so the lack of sightseeing almost worked for me then. After 10 days we returned to our home countries, not having experienced the real India at all.

India came alive for me when I started going to Mysore in 1990. I kept wanting to make the trip to Mysore but it was challenging to arrange because I had a very young school-aged daughter and there was concern about her schooling if she were to travel with me. At that time, no one even thought to travel to India with children. We eventually arranged for her to spend weekdays with her pre-school 'mother' and weekends with her father while I was in Mysore. I stayed in Mysore for six weeks.

After coming home I returned to Mysore and stayed for six months. It became clear that Mysore was my spiritual home.

That kind of moving away is a lot to ask of your husband and children, but I felt like the answers to the questions of life were coming to me now. It felt good to be there. I felt quiet and for the first time in my life, I felt no racism, at least not the violent kind I was used to.

MYSORE

Deep down I knew I needed to study long-term with Guruji, in Mysore. He had a deep understanding of Bhakti; love, devotion and service to God. He truly lived a *spiritual life*. It showed in everything that he did. I truly felt that the universe presented me with a teacher who would guide me from darkness to light; "Asatoma Sat Gamaya". So although I had beautiful little children and a very nice husband, I had a full, rich life with all the elements that I should've and could've wanted from a life - the pursuit of the unknown was pulling at me.

Who am I and what is this life?

ॐ असतो मा सद्गमय ।
तमसो मा ज्योतिर्गमय ।
मृत्योर्मा अमृतं गमय ।
ॐ शान्तिः शान्तिः शान्तिः ॥

Om Asato Mā Sad-Gamaya,
Tamaso Mā Jyotir-Gamaya,
Mrtyor-Mā Amrtam Gamaya,
Om Shāntih Shāntih Shāntih.

Lead me from unreal to real, from dark to light, from death to immortality.

My first trip to Mysore began with a two day lay-over in Europe due to bad weather. When we finally landed in Mumbai, my eyes opened wide and I got a face full of smells, sights and sounds that my senses had never experienced before. No-one mentioned the rivers of open raw sewage that lie between the domestic and the international airports. But there they were.

Despite the gruesome realities, the vibrancy of that big insane city pushed me into an intense excitement. I had a massive adrenaline rush, I was stimulated beyond belief and wanted to know what lay beyond those murky rivers and the pungent smell of garbage. But I really had to stay focused and on point. My 5'6" might seem short at home, but here I was tall, and those who were shorter kept slip-sliding in front of me by going to the side of me first. So after some time I became watchful and attentive, since it was the only way that I would make it to the airline counter without being way-laid.

We were shifted from one line to another, again and again. Once we got through all the official lines, there were the money exchange people and the taxi people. I finally figured out how to get to the domestic airport with the help of a foreigner that I met on the plane from Europe. He had lived in India for the past 20 years and helped me find an official government taxi with a good price. I did not know what that meant at the time.

Inside the taxi I am wide-eyed and marveling at the sights, sounds and most overwhelming, the smells. The smells of India really hit you. You not only smell them, you feel them, you taste them, whether you want to or not. It is salty and sticky and it makes you want to jump and shout. This is funky, made me think of the *p'funk, un-cut funk,* days!!!

I kept thinking - the holiest place on the planet? How could this be? I thought Cleanliness and Godliness are supposed to go together! But then again in India the mundane and the spiritual co-exist in a magical way.

When I got to the domestic airport, it looked like something that had been quarantined several years ago and reopened on a limited basis for 'special needs' and emergency situations. It was a *hot mess*, then I discovered that I had a six hour layover before the flight to Bangalore. And then there was the toilet situation. If you have never seen the *hole in the floor toilet*, it can be shocking!

This was not my first trip to India. When I traveled with the meditation ashram group we were briefed and over-briefed about the toilet situation in India.

Calls Of Nature 101. Rule 1 – always have a bottle of water with you and a cloth for wiping, as well as sanitizer. Both the cloth and the liquid are very important. This is major…in the old days at least one stall in the women's washroom would have a western toilet and the other 4 to 6 would be a hole in the floor, ceramic pan, with a place for your feet, but nevertheless a hole in the ground! There was always a lady there to hand the foreigners some sort of paper, that felt like wax paper to sort of wipe yourself with, in the event that you were not familiar with the bucket of water method. It is truly an adventure when you are coming from the West. We are used to sitting on a toilet, now here you are squatting in a yoga pose while you are relieving your body. On one hand you might think this is primitive but it is far more natural than sitting on a toilet seat to release because the squatting position allows the body to fully relax and release completely.

The fact that this is a practice so foreign to us in America, can have an effect on you. There was a lady on the plane with me traveling from Washington, DC. She had to go to the toilet but when she went inside, just the mere sight of the hole in the floor made her turn around - walk out. Later at the taxi line, she said she did not have to use the toilet anymore and rode all the way to Bangalore from Mumbai without having to go to the toilet!

Okay, finally we are ready for take-off. After an hour or so of flying, we began our descent to Bangalore. Seeing the city from the sky early in the morning was enchanting. Bangalore is a big city but we landed in a very small airport and had to walk a short distance to get to the terminal. It was a quaint little terminal, but of course now that has changed as India has emerged as one of the world's fastest-growing economies. We were greeted by a beautiful woman, in a gorgeous silk brocade sari, she hands us each a rose and welcomes us to *Bangalore, The Garden City.*

We wait and watch as the luggage is hand-carried from the plane and then carefully placed onto the carousel. It is a very old, slow-moving carousel that looks like antique but is actually modern machinery.

It was very humid when we arrived and we could smell mildew which seemed to cover the city and penetrate everything. It felt like it was seeping into my pores. All I knew was that *I DID NOT* want this pungent smell to infuse my soul. I suddenly felt myself close down, but before I could make further mental calculations, my heart took an unexpected turn; I started beaming as the essence of India began to touch me. Suddenly out of nowhere I could hear a tambourine and the sweet sound of a flute, there was a boy in a costume with a lot of little accessories including incense, it was fascinating. We were told that it was some sort of Krishna worship and I realized that in India *closing down* is not an option.

My first trip to Mysore by taxi from Bangalore airport cost me around Rs650. The driver was pleasant but did not speak English and I did not speak *Kannada*, the local language of the people in the state of Karnataka. We made up a sign language for the four hour journey.

At this stage of the journey I had been awake for so long that I was beyond tired. I was truly in the zone of the unknown and I was feeling off-centre, trying to mentally adjust and figure out where my head was at ....it was *way out there.*

But this land filled with mysticism, enchantment and tranquility would not let me sleep, and I was not about to miss out on even one inch of the ride. Actually it is a good thing that there was no one in the vehicle speaking English, because I found myself speechless and wanting to immerse myself in the kaleidoscope that was all around us. I needed to simply experience it, and not intellectually dissect it.

Although it was early morning it still took us almost one and a half hours to get out of the Bangalore city limits. So many rivers of sewage and rivers of people. There were cows on the roads and then more people. There were temples all around and more people. There were small quiet villages and towns and more people. Bicycles and more people. Small cars and more people. Buses and more people. Big trucks and more people. Pigs and more people. Goats and more people. Rickshaws and more people and people and people and people.

Everywhere you turned there were vendors. In India, there are layers upon layers of everything. There is so much color that you start to develop an appreciation for the basic black and white, but that is only because, like everything else, once you learn to be fully conscious and value the colorful onslaught, your vision changes. And change is good.

Eventually we came across the many men and sometimes women wearing orange robes. Are they Sadhus, Sages, Gurus, you wonder. Are they fake, are they real? You begin to delve into the degrees of *holiness* and what that means. After years I learned there are holy men and women, who have renounced society and the world and live on the outside and do their spiritual practices living life in the upper *chakras*.

There are also the temple priests who are often house holders: they can be married; they live a life in service to God they teach from the scripture and ancient text and act as spiritual guides and perform most temple ceremonies.

I also became acquainted with auto-rickshaw drivers. The rickshaw drivers that I have known during my 30 years in India have all come from poor backgrounds. They are usually hard workers and do everything they can do to provide for their families. The rickshaws are all over the place. They are where they should and shouldn't be at the same time, and will always help a foreigner out for a few extra rupees.

They generally know a little English and will take you to shop where the locals shop. The many drivers I have come to know are very honest, friendly and helpful, but my relationship with these men is restricted to Mysore and Mysore is not only a gem in India, but a testament to the times when people were really trying to live in balance and follow some of the rules of life which have a deep yogic thought, and belief.

So back in the traffic, the roads are a separate entity unto themselves. Horrible roads with lumps and bumps and holes like craters, wide and deep.

The poor three wheelers have such a hard time on the roads. If the road conditions were better the auto-rickshaws would last longer and I also believe that the drivers would last longer. It is a classic example of a burn-out job, the fumes poison the drivers, the lungs are destroyed, then all the bouncing around and shaking rips apart the insides. This is one of those jobs that could not exist in a place like the US because the health risks are too great. But in India driving a rickshaw is simply a way for a lot of people to support their families. And they do this work in the spirit of service with very humble hearts, and like many other trades, the drivers pass the business on to their sons for generations to come.

In the old days there were very few privately owned cars in Mysore. For the most part, the roads were full of jeeps, jeep-like vehicles and the slow moving tank that is the Ambassador. There were one or two Japanese cars and some mini-cars that were manufactured in India, as well as bicycles, scooters, and motor cycles. A cacophony of activity!

Indian roads are dominated by tank-like buses and massive trucks colorfully painted with memorable sayings, religious iconography and slogans, and the omni-present *Horn Please*, as well as decorative artwork. The one thing to remember about Indian traffic is to blow your horn and then the largest, pushiest vehicle has the right of way.

I would never attempt to drive in India. My first time in a vehicle was definitely scary, but over the years I have learned little tricks to mentally survive! The roads are now much improved and the trips are sometime relaxing, and this was partly caused by Silicon Valley moving in to Bangalore and changing so much about the road between Bangalore and Mysore.

There is, still now, a cornucopia of the animals on the Bangalore-Mysore road; cows, bullocks, dogs, goats, pigs, horses and in Mysore every once in a while I see elephants and the occasional camel transported down to Mysore for an event and never returned to his home. If animals are on the road and they get tired they will just stop, plop themselves down and the traffic has to go around them. It is jaw-dropping, one of those things about India that I just love because where could this happen and people be so calm about it? People yell and scream about a lot of things but the animals taking a rest in the middle of the road during rush hour is a fact of life that is simply accepted. It is almost like a gift from the universe to slow every one down and give everyone the opportunity to exhale, release, relax and be present.

There is not much open countryside between Bangalore and Mysore. The road is lined with small villages and small towns, temples, ashrams, universities, factories and farms. This part of South India is a manufacturing zone for silk and hand-made toys sugar cane, and cement.

When I first started traveling to Mysore, we drove on a frightening two-lane road which could take 4 to 5 hours. When we took that old road, the drivers all knew the perfect stops (for foreigners) and we would have a delicious big Indian meal and wonderfully aromatic Indian spiced tea, with lots of milk and sugar. It did not matter if at home you were vegan, when you came to mother India you drank milk, tea with sugar and loved every drop of it!

The drivers knew all the places for bottled water and the best toilet spots for foreigners. It was fun. You hopped back in the car and started the drive towards Mysore. The adrenaline started to pump, the driver started to beep the horn to pass the big trucks and the truck drivers would stick their arms out saying, "No, No! don't pass me now!" My driver would start to toot his horn even more, indicating that he wanted to pass and finally the truck would wave him on, and we are on our way to Mysore;

On the Road Again.

Today, the new four lane highway is one of the many prides of the South, as it connects things in a way that have never been connected before. India also has smooth 6-lane highways, expressways and toll roads now. But during my first, visit, the road was under construction and had been under construction for many years. I have photos of women working on the roads in saris carrying stones on the tops of their heads, and men breaking stones by hand with hammers. It reminded me of *The Flintstones* a comedy cartoon about prehistoric people that we watched on TV as kids, except this was real, this is how it was done.

Once the *Silicon Valley* money came, the big machines came and the work that had been in progress for many years was done almost overnight. Café Coffee Day came first, the next thing I knew, in came the big names...Mac Donald's, Subway, KFC and, and Baskin and Robbins a lot of the good old restaurants got demolished to make way for the highway.................**OUCH!!!**

Today it is an easy ride. Café Coffee Day has a clean modern bathroom and right next door is one of the best Indian Restaurants, IndraDanush on the trek between Bangalore and Mysore.

Not everything has changed. You can still see the Hindi Film Studio along the road. India's love of billboards is on full display on the Bangalore-Mysore Road to attract your attention. The moment you start to see the huge towering signs for the hotels and silk shops in Mysore, you realize that you are getting close, maybe only one hour left to go.

Yes the colorful billboards, I immediately start to think about what I will do when I get there.

Besides being filled with historic palaces, Mysore is home to the most beautiful bird sanctuary at *Karanji Lake* which is also a small playground for many crocodiles. The city also has many prestigious Universities, a government-run *Ayurvedic college*, as well as Sanskrit colleges and the famed *Jagamohan Palace, Yoga Shala,* where the great Sage and Yoga Master, *Krishnamacharya* taught, both *Sri. Pattabhi Jois* and *Sri. BKS Iyengar.* Mysore has many *sacred temples* and close to *Melkote*, with a wild life sanctuary and a Sanskrit library and college that attracts scholars from all over the world. In the very center of Mysore is Devaraj Market, a spectacular, traditional open air market.

Mysore has a very strong *Hindu Brahmin* community, however it is home to *Muslims, Buddhists, Christians, Jains, Sikhs* and others.

Thousands of students travel to Mysore yearly to practice Yoga. They come from all over the world. They come to study the original ancient form of yoga believed to be based-on the sacred text, The Yoga Korunta. They come for the discipline and for the experience of being with the great Master, they are on pilgrimage. You see these yoga students at all the airports in India, in New Delhi, Chennai, Mumbai, and Bangalore. "One by one they come", was one of Guruji's daily sayings.

Hearts filled with love wanting to learn, to be healed, seeking salvation, inner peace and guidance, wanting to surrender to the philosophical mythological path of yoga.

My first visit to Mysore was a real eye-opener! It is clean and quiet. It is a University town, it is often compared to Cambridge, Massachusetts. But what really stood out for me was the warm generous spirit of the people, readily inviting you into their homes, willing to take you to visit the historical sites and happy to explain the traditions and culture - Just like in Cambridge.

On this first visit, one of the other yoga students advised me to go either to the *Southern Star Hotel* or the *Metropole Hotel.* I chose the Metropole an old British-built hotel, that looked as though it had been fabulous in its hey-day, but those days were long gone. The Metropole was a majestic building with huge verandas, large rooms with mahogany poster beds, extra-large bathrooms with claw foot bathtubs that you had to step up on a stool to step into. In addition, the hotel had a huge formal dining room, with blown glass chandeliers, and grand mirrors, which gave an empty feeling because the ceilings were so high. It felt like they forgot to add two floors.

A few of us yoga students would meet there at the end of the week on Fridays. It was the one day that we could eat a slightly later dinner since there was no early bedtime for an early practice the next day. On weekends we always planned little trips to temples nearby so that we could return early enough to step back into the routine, discipline of the work. It was beautiful.

Back in those days my practice was rigorous. I started out from the Metropole:

3.00am I AM awake, I take a shower, I complete my morning meditation. I am ready to go to class.

It is pitch black outside, no lights were on. Most mornings there was a power-cut, as was, and still is, very common in India. The electricity had failed hours ago and the batteries of power back-up units are very weak, however my body, mind, and spirit feel relaxed. It is so quiet that you can hear yourself think. I felt so free, peace seemed to be all around me.

*I walk through the city that really feels like a village at this time of the morning. There are still a few stars out although the change is seconds away and the moon is positioning itself, making room for the sun. The chorus of birds and insects are tuning up for the **Sunrise Service**, the smells oscillate from pungent to sweet.*

The sounds of temple bells and prayers slowly start to fill the air. The awakening of the world is in full gear but the quiet follows me to the Yoga shala driveway and I can hear a few students breathing in the room.

Guruji recites his morning prayers very softly. I enter, go upstairs to get my mat and leave my gear. Others enter, in 3 minutes, 12 students totally fill the small shala - Guruji takes his position in the center front and starts the invocation:

न्दे गुरुणां चरणारविन्दे	vande gurūṇām caraṇāravinde
सन्दर्शित स्वात्म सुखाव बोधे ।	sandarśita svātma sukhāvabodhe ꠰
निः श्रेयसे जाङ्गलिकायमाने	niḥśreyase jāṅgalikāyamāṇe
संसार हालाहल मोह शांत्यै ।।	saṃsāra hālāhala mohaśāntyai ꠰꠰
आबाहु पुरुषाकारं	ābhāhu puruṣākāram
शंखचक्रासि धारिणम् ।	śaṅkha cakrāsi dhāriṇam ꠰
सहस्र शिरसं श्वेतं	sahasra śirasam śvetam
प्रणमामि पतञ्जलिम् ।।	praṇamāmi patañjalim ꠰꠰
Aum	

Again, the sound of the breath comes deep, rich and soothing. Guruji's *Shakti,* his transmission of energy, is nourishing our souls. We are deep in the meditation, it is so natural and we are in another world, the world of the unknown, and it feels good. It is silent. The Master observes, adjusts, and aligns but only when necessary, allowing the energy to flow. *Ashtanga* yoga is a very humbling practice - it is meditation in motion.

With each breath we go deeper and deeper inside. Although you know that people are there, you don't see them, but on an energetic level you feel the presence of the Guru as he connects us all and we become one. The power of the breath fills the soul, the heart opens and the practice begins. All the senses become calm and quiet as we retreat inside. Joy takes the soul into ecstasy. It reminds me of that old Black Spiritual:

The Rapture being with God.

Guruji is walking around the room making adjustments, saying a word or two from time to time, but the softness in this cement room feels like the womb of Mother Earth. Inhale, exhale, breathe. The glorious sound of the breath. Six days a week, two moon days a month, ladies holiday, off. That was the deal, and you were expected to commit three months each year of solid practice in Mysore.

When I first arrived at the Ashtanga Yoga Institute, there were 8 students in the room, then 10 and then 12. One year I came and there were only 6 students there. The practice was extremely intense and that room had been filled with yoga students for more than 60 years. Yoga was in the walls and in the carpet that lay on the cement floor, it was powerful energy: pure *shakti.* This was really it, un-cut Yoga, not for the masses, but for the love of Yoga.

We did not have ideal living conditions and, as I have explained, it was not easy to get to Mysore. But it was the place that you came when you wanted to practice "traditional yoga" with a Master who, by that time, had spent his life in devotion to God and Guru. He did not fix it to make it easier for the Western mind-set and we were all grateful to be in his presence.

I spent over a decade practicing in that Lakmishi Puram Shala, ten of the most beautiful years of my life. At times I would come twice a year because I knew there was something extremely special about the whole experience, the ritual, the discipline, and I just wanted to sit at the feet of the Guru. Although he did not talk a lot he was like a mantra, he was energy-based, not word-based. He moved in grace and joy, and that is what we showed up for, when we didn't have money for anything else we still came to Mysore for yoga. Our involvement was 100 percent and the rewards were 200 percent.

I recall Guruji's wife saying to me one day, "You are all our children," and that is how we felt when we were in Mysore with them.

Guruji did not speak perfect English but he had key words and phrases. "Practice practice practice," "All is coming" and he exuded an aura of humble, loving patience, of living in balance with God and nature. He had an incredible smile and was always upbeat. He loved to make jokes and disseminate joy. If he saw you struggle, he would help adjust you into the position, breathe with you, connect to your breath, support you with his breath and, through his energy, transform your breathing. He was very grounded, with a strong male energy, yet he had the warmth and gentleness of female energy. He embodied both as he adjusted you in a pose.

Through him we realized that the breath is the ruler of life and the Universe. Inhale deeply, exhale slowly, feel life as it rushes into your veins. The breath gives us energy, consciousness, rhythm, soul. With the breath we can even take away the blues. We can get by without a lot of things in life, but not the breath.

I remember a story.... of a disciple asking a Swami:

"Sir, what is the proper way to breathe?"

The Swami says with a big smile on his face, "You are breathing....."

"YES." The disciple responded, "Yes Sir, I am breathing."

The Swami says, "This is Proper Method....."

His smile was even larger now, his eyes shining like stars.

The disciple looked confused. "But Sir, I thought and have always been told that there is a proper method."

The Swami says, "Your age?"

"Sir, I am 48."

The Swami responds, smiling, hands in a prayer position, "48 years breathing daily practice. This is proper method. Keep things in life simple...be happy... have joy..... BE LOVE."

Ashtanga Yoga can be physically challenging at times. Many people who come to practice in Mysore are ex-dancers, ex-gymnasts who move with a lot of grace and ease. But Guruji always managed to find the one person in the class who was struggling. In Colorado, on one of his international teaching trips, I observed Guruji work with a very large over weight man, who was also very tall, he always stayed in the back of the room. Guruji moved him to the front, and lovingly worked with him on every single pose. I watched this man over a short period of time become happy, lose weight, and feel included and loved.

I sometimes felt alone in class in Mysore, like in US, since there were very few people of color in his class, so I often felt like the odd ball, and Guruji would give me an adjustment and then sit next to me on the floor he always made sure that we knew that we were a part of him.

I loved his simplicity. He lived in a small house and went about on a scooter. He had the generosity and humility to get up, even a little earlier than most so he could iron his wife's sari for the day. The story is that theirs was a love marriage. Married more than 60 years, and together every day and night. He always praised and honored her, her energy, her laughter and her light. She was as much a part of the shala and the teachings as he was. She was his precious jewel and he held her close to his heart.

It was sad to move away from Lakshmipuram, but Guruji had some new ideas and not only wanted, but needed, a new larger space to teach in. Yoga practitioners from all over the world started to flock to Mysore like birds, migrating to the south during winter months to be fed the ancient unaltered teachings of Ashatanga Yoga.

Yoga became popular and now has become part of the mainstream culture. In 1993 *PBS broadcast* a documentary special about various mind-body therapies. This marked a major turning point for the image of Yoga and it shed new light on the entire alternative health and preventive health care movement, including Yoga and meditation. Shortly thereafter many 'Pop Culture Magnets' openly endorsed Yoga as part of their daily exercise regime. Then before long pharmaceutical drug companies were hiring models to perform Yoga postures, sometimes in ads on TV, to sell their products.   *OUCH!!!*

Some purists believed that the crossover into popular culture meant the end of Yoga, and for others, it heralded a new beginning. *Yoga* had a new attitude, it had been redefined, reinvented by the talk show hosts and exercise gurus. There was a brief moment or two when it was considered one of the fastest growing industries in America.

There were times when I felt like the counter-culture, alternative lifestyle hippies like myself had to go into silence. We had to become the

Spook Who Sat By The Door.

It felt like our world of Yoga and meditation was becoming obsolete and infiltrated. Before long people started to practice Yoga for a whole host of reasons.

Sometimes people came to Mysore because they wanted a Yoga vacation, or then there was the *I-want-a-boyfriend or I-want-a-girlfriend-Yoga.* At one point there were lots of parties going on hosted by the young Yoga students, Mysore started to seem like Goa - a town in India where all the European and American kids come for night life - but Guruji's grandson nipped that one right in the bud and said, no! no! no! But of course there were, and continue to be, extremely sincere and respectful Yoga students.

I befriended a woman from the US. She came to practice Yoga at the Shala *on the mat* but wound up rolling up her mat up and living her life in service.

It was the year that the new Shala opened in Gokulam and there were hundreds of new students. Originally from Hawaii, she had lived in New York and San Francisco. Educated in one of the more prestigious universities in the US, she had a great job, and started practicing Yoga in San Francisco with a wonderful teacher. It seemed she was *seeking* and decided to come to India to practice at the Shala.

She was very devoted to her personal Yoga practice. In the Shala, there is a system, a process - an obsession some might say - the time, the spot, everything associated with the practice, you know what I mean if you have practiced in that room.

She was totally dedicated to it. Nothing took her away from the practice.

She was also overwhelmingly taken by the beauty of the culture and the people. We would occasionally take day trips and if it interfered with her Yoga timing, she would not participate. For most students that is normally how it plays out when you first come to Mysore. The discipline regarding the practice is very important.

But something different happened to her .... She had an experience while visiting the Devaraj market in downtown Mysore that completely changed her life. She helped a little girl in need who was sick. She took her to the doctor and found out the little girl actually lived on the street with several other children, babies, mothers, fathers, grandparents and so on. She went back to check on the little one daily and found that before long she was operating a street program that eventually through hard work became an orphanage.

She worked with anyone and everyone who was in need, people with leprosy, tuberculosis, cancer, HIV and AIDS. She worked with those who were crippled, and with the destitute. Sometimes she was purely there to give the children a big hug. This was all done with her not speaking Kannada or them speaking English. It shows that acts of compassion and love do not require the spoken word.

At times she would organize yoga students to help, but the local people from Gokulam, Swamiji Jamanagiri from the Chamundi Hill Shiva Temple, Dr. Gurubasavaraj from JSS Ayurvedic Hospital were great resources for her and helped her establish *Operation Shanti* a California-based non-profit organization to help the poorest and neediest in Mysore to rise above their circumstances, get an education, regain some status and a place in society; all opportunities that would normally be inaccessible.

Operation Shanti - directly helps to improve the lives of exploited, at-risk destitute children and the forgotten, suffering elderly. To this day the organization provides food, shelter, medical services and education.

Operation Shanti, is inspiring. I have had the marvelous opportunity to work with many of the students whose lives were profoundly changed by the program. Their *road map* has been completely reversed, and one can immediately see joy in their eyes and feel the peace and love in their hearts.

Aum shanti aum.

As for my own life, it was becoming increasingly clear to me with every trip, that it was more and more difficult and challenging for me to return to New York.

My children are all grown up and have their own families. Life there is of course so expensive that just the fiscal logistics of being in Mysore made more sense. I spent so much time in Mysore, that Mysore felt like home.

New York was about work and friends. I was very attached to my students in my small shala and very involved with the students at the high school in lower Manhattan, but I saw that I could live deeply and quietly in Mysore, around beauty, and people of like mind, and maybe people with similar beliefs.

I began to make the shift wherein India became my home.

DHYANA

ध्यानहेयास्तद्वृत्तयः ।

Dhyānaheyāstadvṛtayaḥ.

Meditation in Beauty

All mental disturbance is healed by meditation. --Yoga Sutra II.11

One of the life lessons that I have truly learned and experienced is that if you honor life, life will honor you. In Mysore, I had times when I felt like I was in heaven or someplace that is very close to it.

The Ashtanga Yoga shala, that was located in Lakshmipuram, moved to *Gokulam* in 2002. Gokulam was a small sleepy community on the outskirts of Mysore. Guruji woke it up. Since then it has grown, not only with large houses but also with more yoga shalas. There are meditation and healing centers, organic cafes and lots of foreigners on pilgrimage to study the undiluted teachings of the great sages of the ancient path of yoga.

I eventually moved to Gokulam to be close to Guruji and the Ashtanga Yoga Community. I lived in several communities in and around Mysore but now that I was spending most of the year in India, I wanted and needed to be close to the Guru and his family. I leased a beautiful house from Guruji's daughter Saraswati. This is the home where Saraswati raised her children. It has been remodeled, and a Yoga Shala added. The Shala is on the second floor and its entrance is an exterior stair case. My home is on the first floor.

The shala has kept me right up close to the practice. It was originally added so that mother and son could teach their own classes after they both taught with Guruji in the mornings at the Ashtanga Yoga main shala. Life took its course and after Guruji took Samadhi things changed. Saraswati named the upstairs shala Manasa Saraswatiji and teaches there.

Guruji's only daughter Saraswathi is a remarkable woman, who walks in her father's footsteps, always honoring his name and walking his path. She is priceless, sometimes I will look over at her and she will smile and I see and sense Guruji. When you have her and her devoted son, Sharath in the room together it is magic; he will recite the invocation using the same intricate tones and breath patterns that Guruji used, joy comes over her face, then that majestic smile, and you know in your soul that the journey has begun. They are Guruji's gift to us, his students and the continuation of the lineage of Ashtanga Yoga.

At Manasa Saraswati, class starts at 4:30am six days a week. In the beginning she would join her son at 8:00am at the main shala and teach with him. There was immense love between Saraswati, Sharath and Guruji. They work tirelessly to uphold the tradition of Ashtanga Yoga. Saraswati is held in great esteem; she does her duty, she offers her love, and shares her wisdom to all with a smile on her face.

My mornings were wondrous because of the proximity to Yoga. I take my early morning walk, I go to temple and then to the flower stand to buy garlands and jasmine to offer the main shala and then I head home for my own puja. I have an office on the side entrance of my home which houses a clinic, where I offer *colonics* to western students at the western price (India joke). I also grew *wheatgrass* in my sunny patio and would serve the juice to the Yoga students each and every day.

KUKKARAHALLI LAKE

I love Gokulam and my favorite time of day is of course, early early mornings and my walk to Kukkarhalli Lake about 3 or 4 kilometers away. I walk back and forth, twice a day, at sunrise and then again at sunset. It is God's house and my sanctuary, and its beauty gives me peace. My heart feels so much love at times, tears of joy travel down my face. I have never felt so much love as I feel in this place. The birds and insects are the *rhythm nation* and the wind is the voice of God.

My walk to the lake takes me through Gokulam. Then there is a small village that I walk through to get to the lake. If I said it once I will say it again and maybe a million times again, it is like heaven, the smell of incense and flower blossoms the sound of bells ringing and the holy prayers of Hindus, Muslims, Sikhs, *Jains*, Christians. Ghee lamps burning, hearts and souls opening, and God greeting some of us with the sun and at the same time saying good night to others with the moon.

When I begin my walk, it is quiet outside, still dark and there is a soft energy. I mentally repeat to myself Lord Ram's name:

Aum Shri Rama

Jai Rama

Jai Jai Rama

I slowly start to enter another plane of consciousness, but it is okay because I am walking up God's highway. I get through the village and there are cows being washed, cow dung being collected, cow stables being cleaned. The cow in India is sacred, the holy cow that nourishes and protects us and gives us life.

The cow is honored like the Guru. In fact the cow is also Guru and when I see the love, the honor, the respect that is bestowed upon these beautiful animals daily, I feel that special connection we all have to each other - we are one.

I always feel like a bride when I reach the lake. The entrance is a long aisle with massive tall trees on each side, some reach to the other side forming a beautiful archway. The insects, the birds, the bees, the toads and the frogs are singing humming buzzing and making sounds that create the most natural rhythms that sooth and nourish the soul. Nature's orchestra is in concert performing early morning prayers.

I love Kukkarahalli Lake. I am told in the course of a day over 1,000 birds visit the lake. The most impressive is the Sarus Crane, the world's tallest flying bird - the male can stand 6 feet tall. There are 3 recognized species that live on the Asian sub-continent, and are protected through both the Indian culture and the great Hindu religion. However, loss of wetlands, crop fertilizers, and pollution has placed them in danger.

The lake has unique sounds, as well as unique smells. When the trees bloom, the fragrance is sweet and where the water is standing, the stench is sour. Again, we experience that bitter and sweet edge that is so common to India.

I slowly start my journey around the lake. There are joggers, walkers, meditators, yoga students and small yoga classes, people playing bad-minton, people stretching and weight training. There are priests clutching malas, chanting Sanskrit verses, and workers in meditation. There are people there, who are just taking in the beauty of the lake and fishermen who make their living from this lake. It is sadly, even a place where some have chosen to end their lives. The lake is a full circle, representing life, embracing birth and death. Every time I am there, I stop and inhale deeply. The sun warms and soothes my body. The breath lubricates my soul. Nature is God's sanctuary.

I have spent so much time walking around the lake, that I have made incredible friends there. One day I met one of the walkers who just happened to be an employee of the university. On the second time around she invited me to her home for tea. Once she learned that I chant Sanskrit verses, she chanted such beautiful verses, and made such a wonderful cup of tea and as the conversation started to flow, we realized that we had mutual friends from Kenya. I was so touched by the whole experience, that the next time I saw her on a walk, I thanked her again. She was also happy - we sat in silence for about twenty minutes then we both stood there, held each other's hands and promised to stay in touch at the soul level. That was many years ago now when we see each other on our journey around the lake, we touch our hearts lower the head and feel the joy for each other as we move around the magnificent lake in an un-rehearsed state of rapture. I can still hear my Grandma Peyton say "touch your heart feel God."

When I got home from the lake each day I thought, in 'God's sanctuary' beautiful things always happen.

India has taught me that when the heart opens, the honey of life will flow in through unforgettable experiences and a great teacher.

SWAMIJI JAMANAGIRI

Jamanagiri Swamiji is the *resident* Sādhu at the cave Shiva temple next to the *Nandi Bull* at Chamundhi Hills, above Mysore. He has been in residency since the early nineties and follows a long line of great Swamiji's. I met him maybe his first or second year in residency at the cave.

I heard that there was a new Swami in the cave and this was important to me. As a student I always spent time in the holy places: The Nandi Bull statue in Chamundi Hill's was one of those very special places we would go often and there was always the *excitement*, the elation associated with the little cave temple next door to the huge black stone bull, with the mysterious sādhu inside. When I heard that a new person, a new mystic, was there, I naturally wanted to see him. At the time, just meeting a true sādhu, a person living with no attachments and in devotion to God was a big deal for me.

So I got a vehicle and headed up to the cave. I really did not have anything to ask Swamiji. I did not want anything. I simply wanted go and see. I asked the priest at the Nandi Bull about the new Swami and they pointed me in the direction of the cave. The opening was clear but I was a little nervous so I walk over to the platform in front. I glance in and I see that someone is inside.

My heart starts to race a little. I am not sure why I am so emotional. WOW... So I sit on the stone fence that separates the Bull Temple from the Shiva Cave Temple and inhale deeply and slowly exhale.

The Sādhu emerges from the cave, red cloth, dark skin, waist length matted locks, long beard, 4'5" or 4'6" and 75 to 80 pounds, with his piercing gaze and majestic presence; a perfect National Geographic image. it felt like Sādhu Royalty. I felt good.

Just one look that is all it took.

He retreats back into the cave and I sit for a while longer, and eventually make my way down the hill. We did not exchange any words but the experience was rich and beautiful, beyond words.

As I made my way home, I realized that I was no longer anxious. In fact a real peace came over me and that evening as I started my evening prayers, *Aum Namah Shivaya* rolled off my tongue. I chanted to Lord Shiva for a couple of hours.

My dreams were very vivid that night and in the morning I found myself still chanting Lord Shiva's name.

I did not visit the cave again on that trip to Mysore. There was no need to. The movement of energy, the Shakti that I felt at that first meeting was so powerful, my battery was **charged.**

One thing that I learned from Guruji is that the presence of the Guru, the holy person, is all one may need from time to time. Words are not necessary. In the presence of devotion, *there is peace, love and joy.*

Now I spend time at the cave temple every time that I am in Mysore. I love the cave. A lot of times I just go and we just sit in silence, it is amazing. A few years ago I began going up to the cave to hear Swamiji recite Rudrams in the evenings. Before long I was attending his early morning puja. Swamiji would tell beautiful stories about Lord Ram, Lord Hanuman, Chamundeswari, Chamundi Hills......

Sometimes the foreign yoga students would gather there and they wanted to understand his chosen path, why? when? where is your family? Swamiji's answer to most questions was devotion, service and love of God. Specifically, he would say:

"Trust is there...

respect is there ...

devotion is there...

peace is there...

joy is there ...

this is the good simple life."

Swamiji has also been my guide for healing my physical body for many years. Shortly after meeting him, I began to have problems with osteo-arthritis, which was a result of a car accident in my early 20s. When these problems started to surface, it caused modifications in my yoga practice and life. I experienced tremendous pain and suffering.

Swamiji also had some physical pain from his time living in and walking across the Himalayas. He had journeyed through the world of Ayurveda, *Pranic Healing* and other natural therapies, he recommended places for me to go to receive natural treatment.

At one time he instructed me to go to the Naturopathic Wellness Center in the middle of the jungle in the south of India, located between Coorg and Mangalore. They believe in treating the whole body, detoxifying the body completely and allowing it to heal itself. No supplements, no herbs and...no tricks. The clinic is nestled in a grove of coconut and banana trees; with the birds and the bees.

One of the main treatments at the clinic is mud baths and baking in the sun. The other therapies are Acupuncture, Ayurvedic treatments and manipulations, the use of cold-water soaks and steam baths. The small private cabins for lodging are made from materials that have been recycled from the area.

It is such a phenomenal setting, you feel as though Mother Earth is reaching out and drawing you into her womb for a spiritual and physical healing.

The doctors are a husband and wife team who work the land themselves and are dedicated to bringing the patients back to health, back to nature. There are many elements on the property that take me back to my childhood on the farm in Oklahoma, never thought I would find myself in India playing and healing in the *sun* and *mud*. *Wow*!

The clinic follows ancient traditions and rituals, using well water, honoring the earth, healing with mud baths, silent therapy and the sacred cow's energy that grounds us to the earth but, elevates our spirits to God and universe. In Hinduism cows are also believed to protect people from negative energy.

My life in Mysore was exceptional…..transcendent. I felt as though I was living in communion with the earth and all of its richness.

SAMADHI

समाधिसिद्धिरीश्वरप्रणिधानात् ।

Samādhisiddhirīśvarapraṇidhānāt.

Absorption in the Infinite.

Music as the ether.

M y gurus have been many, and come from all walks of life they have been powerful and very inspirational. I believe that the term *guru* includes all those people who influenced or changed your life, for any given moment. I have mentioned several in these pages but I am not done and I think that as long as I live I will continue to learn and grow through the Guru disciple relationship.

So guess what here are *three* more major influences in my life. Those who gave me life and in many ways unknowingly guided me on the path of yoga, so that I could collect the very shattered pieces of my soul, that had been tormented and dissected by racism segregation and discrimination. Somehow through either their art, their love and compassion for life or their desire to elevate the soul, they claimed a piece of my heart and unknowingly became my teachers.

They are great, they are grand, they are gurus:

I include the prophecy of the revolutionary poet and musician Mr. Gil Scott Heron, the quintessential raw mysticism of Turiyasangitnanda; the great Alice Coltrane; and the power of Motown. Motown was like a force of nature that expanded the voice of Negro Spirituals and the desire for Freedom, Peace and Love - from the fields, and plantations in America to the Black churches into the dancing shoes of our generation.

YOGA CIVIL RIGHTS AND MUSIC HEALS

There is no exact record of the number of *African slaves* that were sold and crossed the Atlantic. The estimates range from 11 to 50 million.

After a long work day, slaves would sometimes get together and sing songs that were sometimes just moans, prayers and affirmations. The songs were sad, and expressed the oppression and pain that they endured. I believe that out of this pain, came the birth of the Blues, Gospel and Jazz. *Call and response* was also a practice of these slaves, much like the *Kirtan* and chanting of *Bajans* in India. The goal was similar - to unite the body and mind, free the spirit and bring joy. I truly believe that so many stories of life are told through music and through sound, the evolution of the earth and history of the world has been told through song. Sound and song are a pleasant way to learn and sound is a vital tool in yoga also.

In 1975, I was in under-grad school in San Diego, California. My dear friend Jarue, who was still living in Northern California calls. He says, "*I have the best gift for you. We are going to the concert of your life, when we arrive you can open the gift.*"

I started to get a little excited. We always remained close, but at times the communication was not consistent, and this was one of those times. "Who are we going to see?"

"I am not going to tell you. I'm driving down and I will be there in about 14 hours."

I said OK, hung up the phone, and thought that we must be seeing Aretha.

At that point in my life, I was all about Aretha Franklin *the queen of soul, and:* the feel good music of Motown whose lyrics nourished my thoughts, I was definitely a Motown girl, R/B, , funk, blues, gospel. Nina Simone was my jazz moment - I worshipped her.

I took my time because Jarue was always late. But no, for the first time ever, he was on time, and he was hurrying me up. I dawdled, making myself all cute, making sure my afro looked right, while he was saying "let's get going!" I was a little surprised.

I opened the bathroom door, he was standing there and handed me an album with a beautiful woman on the cover. I looked and said "Oh this is John Coltrane's wife, Alice. Wow.....she plays the harp *Journey into Satchidananda. Great title!*"

"The plan was to go to the concert first and then show you the album, but come on, let's listen to it now. He was so excited, saying, "We are actually seeing the great Pharaoh Sanders with some of the members from the band on this album". He put the album on the record player and came to sit down next to me.

The first track was *Journey to Satchidananda*, a six minute masterpiece. I sat there mesmerized, and everything changed. I had never, ever heard music like this. It felt spiritual. It *is* spiritual music. The music put me into another realm of consciousness. I was without words, my interior tingled with joy, my mind felt at peace, at rest and inner quiet was upon me. It was like a whisper that I could feel.

Every musician on the album is a master. The piece was dedicated to her 'spiritual preceptor,' Swami Satchidananda and her late husband.

I was in love with the music and I played it every day from that moment on.

Jarue and I were off to see Pharaoh Sanders at a place in Redondo Beach called Concerts by the Sea. Most of the musicians from the album were playing with him. I was in a state of rapture; this whole experience was another turning point in my life. I was introduced to another type of music that I knew nothing about. I realized that there is so much power and energy in music, which is why it heals and connects the body mind and spirit. Music goes beyond religion, cast, race, and economics.

I was so inspired by Alice Coltrane's transcendental, spiritual, sacred music, that I wrote a poem. I had never written a poem before. I recited it to Jarue and a few other friends, with *Journey to Satchidnanda* playing in the background and my friend's response was, "You've got to read this in the Black Student Union. You gotta do this... she's motivating you." So I did. I was amazed how strong Coltrane made me feel. The poem went like this:

My skin is black
My Hair is Kinky
My lips are thick
And my hips are wide
I am a Black Woman black as the Night Is Black
Black as the Depths of My AFRICA!!!

From the beginning, I have played her music at every single yoga class that I taught for years. I opened each class with *Journey to Satchidananda* and ended the class meditation with *Carlos Nakai's* Native American flute playing his meditative *Canyon Trilogy*.

Alice Coltrane fused it all; gospel, jazz, blues, soul eastern music and conjured a new meaning to devotional music. Her music included every dimension of sound, it grasped your soul, ignited you spirit, she was inclusive devoted, the embodiment of love, her message seemed so clear,

"let's love each other."

She and her musicians were like gurus, disciples and prophets. Their music tapped the chakras all so gently that the soul and the heart opened. When I listen to that music even now, my energy still rises. Alice Coltrane was a bolt of energy sent from the creator to heal and ignite souls.

That is what she did.

In 2013, I dedicated my recording *Lord Ram* to The Great Sista Alice Coltrane Turiyasangitnanda. She is no longer with us, but her music is her powerful gift to all.

My other teacher was a man who taught us as Black American people to know and understand the depths of who we are. We the direct descendants of slaves, with a complex history we have had and are currently dealing with. He brought intelligence to some of the insanity we were feeling, sanity to some of the confusion and guilt we naturally felt from not being able to make sense of our world.

Gil Scott-Heron, poet, musician, novelist, thinker, leader, prophet was really a peer of mine, just a few years older. In the late 60s Scott Heron was taking a break from Lincoln College to write his first novel while still making music with his brilliant partner, Brian Jackson. As a young student at San Diego State University, we would spend time sitting around the Black Student Union waiting for the next piece of music, waiting for the next word. Ironically, it was a big white house which we called the Black house building.

As kids we had been segregated in every aspect of daily life. We had been brought up during that time when Blacks were not able to go into certain areas of town at certain times of day. We were taught how to act in public so as not to get in any trouble or be hurt. This type of fear and racism stifles human growth. Children can't grow free and strong when intimidated, and in fear for their lives. We had been told as kids, "Look at the White person when you talk to them. Stand tall, speak loudly and clearly, so they will not ask you the same question again... so they will not humiliate you." The command itself was humiliating. We had to walk with a fear of dogs, dogs who are naturally friends to man, were trained to attack us. Don't move, don't smile, say "yes sir, no sir, thank you."

Gil Scot-Heron, a tall, witty and truthful man, wanted to speak out about what we were going through. He sang and wrote without fear of pulling any punches. He told it strong, poetically, forcefully and as it is. In his slow southern majestic Shakespearean voice, he gave us so much strength and energy. He was gifted in being able to observe ills and insanity and see what was actually happening. We would get it.

I would listen to his words and reflect on the days prior to the Civil Rights Movement, the days of the back of the bus, the days of **No Colored Allowed.** I knew the pain of not being treated as equal and it would surface a lot of times. My heart and soul would cry, but his articulation of that reality would push me to work a little harder for peace.

He knew how to break it down and make it plain. We would sit around in the Black Student Union office listening to the words and the soul of the man that I refer to as *"the voice of freedom and change"*. He gave us so much to think about. For many of us he gave the gift of basic understanding which often leads to knowledge and awareness. His vehicle of spoken word, often fused with heavy rhythm and blues, over tones would drive the energy up the spine, piercing the chakras.

He has often been cited as the founding father of rap, but he was much more of a poet, without any interest in commercialism. He drew huge crowds, because his was a voice people would listen to. He had the same anger we all did, but he channeled his anger intelligently, and he sang and talked constantly about what was pulling at him; in the music, on vinyl records.

We all knew his albums and poems word for word. At times he would stop recording. He had, as he said himself, many demons.

The true meaning of the Greek word, prophet, is one who has supernatural powers, a divinity, one who serves as an intermediary of sorts between God and humanity, one who delivers profound knowledge from the other worlds or realms of consciousness. One who delivers a prophecy.

Much of Gil Scott-Heron's prophecy was based on *internal revolution*, as well as political, cultural, social, and economic change. I understood his message to be;

> *know thy self, love thy self, and let history record the truth.*

Being open to the truth often leads one to tremendous opposition and at times, persecution. Scott-Heron himself had a difficult life, he was inordinately talented and gifted. Each spoken and written word of the great Scott-Heron has a tremendous effect, which created a profound revelation. The lyrics of his most celebrated work:

"The Revolution will Not Be Televised",

is a poem of the time combining politics and life.

Other title tracks speak directly to the heart and soul. There was *Small Talk at 125th and Lenox, Pieces of a Man, From South Africa to South Carolina,* and *It's your World.* Each year from 1970 to 2010, there were messages from him. In 1994, many years after my university days and the, *The Revolution will Not Be Televised,* he recorded *Spirits,* my favorite track, *Work For Peace* was released. So beautiful; this piece resonated with my soul.

For almost forty years I watched him. I watched his energy, so alive, always moving the audience, always making us laugh and cry and hope. Even in the last few years when his body started to get weak, his mind stayed strong. He left us early. His body has now gone home, but the spirit, that desire to talk about freedom and peace in the world, will live on and on.....

"Thank you Brother Gil Scott-Heron for giving so many of us your life."

The third major influence for me was a complete music movement - Motown. Feel-good music. It took away all the pain of recrimination. Everyone was moving in joy to their sound. The unity they brought was a huge rip in the separation of whites and blacks. That music was nectar, a recipe for life. To this day, when I listen, my soul shifts into hope and a feeling of goodness.

I read an interview once with Smokey Robinson explaining Motown's cultural impact. He spoke about the '60s and how wonderful it was to be making music but also realizing that they were changing the world and recording history. He mentioned that in the early days, Motown artists went from playing to segregated audiences in the south, to playing in completely integrated audiences where the young black kids and white kids were dancing together and holding hands, with big smiles on their faces. Music heals and Motown played a huge part in soothing the soul and dissolving racial barriers. What Motown did is monumental. It was the 60s and it was a different time.

This was that revolution, that change.…. this was the Man in the Mirror, a new life, a new day.…. it is one of the many doors that open through the magic of sound and poetry, compassion and love.

The Motown Sound embraced all of life. People kept trying to figure out how to reproduce the sound, do we need to go to Detroit? What does one do to sound like that? Do we turn up the bass?. Double up on the drums? People often wondered if the Motown sound came from the air in Detroit, from the earth in and around Detroit. The *Motown Revue would* regularly travel around the country, and the world. So you did not *need the air in Detroit* to make the Motown sound.….! Even as a kid I knew that it was the heart and soul of the artist singing expressing the journey of life with all its ups and downs, in and out's and just how people with a passion for life make music that thrills and heals the soul.

I strongly believe that their sound is spirit-based soul music, that comes from the depths of the souls of artists who can perform and record anywhere, because the spirit is inside. It's spiritual, and it comes from the heart and soul of the artiste who make it happen.

Motown artists knew that their break-through into the white popular music market made them examples for other Black artists seeking broad market acceptance. Motown artists were groomed to represent *The Royal World of Motown,* they were taught to think, act, walk and talk like royalty. Motown dressed their musicians and choreographed the acts to create an elegant presentation style, long associated with the label. The artist development department created the 'perfect image'. The Motown Image.

I once read that Mavis Staples (of the Staple Singers), said that Curtis Mayfield's (a Motown Great) "*Love Songs* would make you fall in love and his Message Songs made you want to go out and do something good for the world." This could be said about all Motown Artists.

Motown made us happy. I danced to this music. I sang to this music. I was proud of this music. The backup sound, the singing-out was natural to me and right out of church. Even rap artists today really come from the Black Church.

These three influences were the rock of my soul:

Turiyasangitananda - State of Pure Consciousness

Mr. Gil Scott Heron - The Prophet

Motown, the feel-good music

The 'Gurus'. Music brings love to the soul, a "let's get together" feeling. Guru will lead you to the light and put you on the right road for a life working for peace, while moving in joy along the way.

TAKING CARE OF YOUR BODY CENTER

My intention was not to solely focus on traditional yoga teachings. There is a plethora of books about Yoga in India and in *the West*. To study *postures,* there are a number of useful books. For many years, I have recommended B.K.S. Iyengar's book, *Light on Yoga* and Sri K. Pattabhi Jois' *Yoga Mala* and *Suryanamaskara.*

Living a life in Yoga is my focus and passion. If only one person out of a million who pick up a yoga mat is willing to do selfless service for humankind, and work on Realization for the soul, then love, peace and happiness - our birth right - is on the rise!

The practice of Yoga teaches us a lot about caring for the body. It begins with learning to move with a conscious mind through observing life and the teachings. We become conscious of who and what we are. The conscious mind perceives the body as the temple that houses the soul. Living in balance we develop body awareness, and a sensitivity where nutrition not only nourishes the body but also nourishes the soul.

I love that old hippie saying "You are what You eat". It makes a lot of sense. That said, there are no rigid rules in yoga as to what we should eat. I have met strict vegetarians and I have met people who drink alcohol and eat meat who are avid yoga practitioners.

In the practice of yoga some of the poses will dictate what you eat so you can operate at your 'optimal level' giving you that lightness to glide and flow from one pose to the next, as well as the lightness that is required for meditation and for living life in the real world. I have seen people who were incessant coffee drinkers, two pack a day smokers, and hamburger eaters become vegetarians and give up their habits. By doing the discipline, your senses will open up and a revolution may take place inside your body. Your body and soul will instruct you as to what is right for you. There is no one size fits all.

The *Sattvic diet*, which a lot of Spiritual people in India follow, has some very simple rules: no animal meats or skins but plenty of legumes, fruits, wheat and herbs - this diet is filled with *prana* that nourishes the body, mind and spirit. The Bhagavid Gita describes the Sattvic diet as "promoting life, virtue, strength, health, happiness and satisfaction". The Sattvic diet is said to bring clarity to the mind. This is said to be the yogi diet.

Some people think that vegetarians have less energy. Not true at all. I have spent most of my life as a vegetarian, a good part of that time I have been Vegan. The past 5 or 6 years I started taking milk in my tea, I think that can easily happen living in India. My energy level even now is unusually high. I require no more than 4 hours of sleep, which is great since I love getting up early around 3:30am or 4:00am in the morning and going to bed at midnight. I am at my best in the softness of twilight and that is when I do most of my reading, writing music and morning meditation. I read scripture in the early morning, it is great especially when I follow it with something silly and funny, something that makes me laugh! It is a wonderful way to start the day. Over the years I have learned to keep everything light and soft. No need to be such a serious yogi or a meditator who does not smile when I think about Guruji, *Pattabhi Jois*. I always think about that majestic smile that gave so much joy and love to so many. Yoga is non-attachment, not a military undertaking.

Meditation, is very important to keep a strong body and a strong healthy mind.

Meditation is a deep state of relaxation where we feel peace and we can commune with God.

In meditation the breath moves in the body like a current of energy, lubricating the muscles and joints energizing the blood cells. We exhale and the breath removes toxins and impurities. Over time we understand that to keep the body healthy, strong and pure meditation is key. The body must be *"Solid As A Rock."*

When fluent in a meditation practice life becomes easy and you will be present every moment, with whatever you are doing, with whomever is in your life.

As an example, when I am with my children and grand children, I am fully there and give them all my attention. If you're not present, people know that only a shell of you is available. Since we're defined by our actions, it is very important to be real and be true to who you are and what you are doing. Only then will your vibration come across and reach another.

Being present tends to eliminate drama. When you are in the moment, you see and feel what is really going on, accept and go with the truth. You are not trying to change anyone. You are working on your own karma and development.

All the talk of the mind/body connection is true. You can't just have the intellect and you can't just have the body. They need to be integrated, whole. Yoga does that. It's a continual growth. We are all a work in progress, even after practicing for more than 40 years. I keep moving forward, stopping, reflecting, inhaling, exhaling and walking with life. The more conscious we are in our breathing, the more in balance and harmony we will feel in our life and with the universe. We are a part of the planet, the trees, all that is around us. To remain grounded, hug a tree, kiss a flower......

Each one of our bodies tells a different story and our bodies will tell us how far we can go, based on our body's unique imprint and rhythm. We should be in a dialogue with our body.

The study of yoga is spiritual. The practice will awaken and align you to the voice from deep within it may take years but the practice will lead you to that internal voice. No we don't have to be athletes to do yoga and get the benefits. Our only job is to awaken our interior.

BKS Iyengar often used props and modified poses so that every one of us could do yoga regardless of our condition. Yoga is truly for the people. There are people in wheelchairs who do yoga. I have done yoga in hospice with people who were dying and with people who were incarcerated, children and gang members housewives and executives, anyone can do yoga. *Yoga Works*, it makes us Happy and brings us to that point of peace simply by breathing and being aware of the breath in the body. So if you've been hurt or are not strong, you can *still* do yoga.

An enlightened person is not a person of 1,000 poses. It's a person who is connected to his or her inner self.

Yoga will strengthen the body eliminate stress and boost the immune system. Studies have shown that vegetarians are half as likely to develop prostate cancer as meat eaters. When I turned 50, I was told to get a colonoscopy. My western doctor in New York said, "Oh you've been a vegetarian since 15? You don't need a test. You are not at all a high risk colon cancer candidate."

Yoga of course, cannot stop aging. We all age. *As my sister says - growing old beats the alternative.*

No matter what age we are, if we access the beauty around us, the beauty becomes part of us. We all spend a lot of time thinking about our own beauty. But as we practice yoga, we start to see the aura of a person. Mother Teresa, in her life of giving, became the essence of beauty. In other words, beauty goes beyond the physical, it is illuminated by acts of the soul. One can see a person's chakra, light, and that illuminates their inner glow. Gil Scott-Heron was such a beautiful man because he was living his own truth, proud and strong. He had his issues, as we all do, but he could access who he really was, share it with others, enjoy himself as he did it, give it back to the world, his message was simple: *Be Yourself. Live your truth.* He created beauty as a poet and musician and lived it, pain and all. **Beauty is the force of your inner vision, your inner drive and your inner love of life.** And it is enhanced with how you give love back out to others.

The truth is real beauty and body elixirs come in one package: **Joy.**

If you have joy, smiles, laughter, music - then you are young, vibrant and connected to the interior life and the soul. You'll find the *joy package* far more lasting and powerful than a lot of expensive creams and surgery, and far more enabling of a connection to others.

LIVING YOUR OWN LIFE

I have lived a life that I envisioned was right for me but, of course, that life reflected some of what I had been raised to live. My family were God-loving people who cared about other people, who were concerned about the welfare of the people in our community and so I took that value and made it my own. Living a life in yoga, for me, meant demonstrating and teaching all the benefits of yoga to those in community, being involved in grass roots activities where people get together to work in shelters and soup kitchens, and help those who are not as blessed as we are. To live a life in yoga is to give, give, give. If that is your inner drive, the actual work you are meant to do will present itself. It is usually your particular talent: it could be teaching math, being a social worker, a nurse, piano teacher, whatever talent you have, that is what you give back to the community. It is where your work feels like joyous service because you are helping our society raise itself. If it is service, you will enjoy it because you will be connected to your work by love.

Yoga today has become 'Hip'. Stars do it. Yuppies do it. There is so much talk about how it can make your body strong and healthy, and help you get in touch with your inner 'self.'

Yoga is an inner commitment to a life of purity, spirituality, and connection with the divine through acts of kindness and love.

Naturally, choosing a life of service means I lived on short money. But the thing about that is one still always has enough.

It really does not take a lot of money to live a good life.

In my travels I have seen so many people live in goodness and joy. The world is made up of people who live simple lives, in simple homes, doing simple good work. I spoke to a village man he told me that daily he goes out in the fields, from sunrise to sunset, and comes home and his wife serves them simple food. But the most wonderful thing for him is when his young son sits on his tummy, and says, "You're the greatest dad in the world."

At this point in my life, "working in the fields for me" is spending more time on my music, playing with my grand children, they are being taught yoga at school and love showing me head stand shoulder stand and back bends. I spend a lot of time with young people, I listen to them and I am **"living, learning and still dancing in the river of life."**

It is their world now. We who came up in the 60s and 70s, the hippies, did what we could to become free from the stringency of the 50s. The color divide is what it is, we still have a big job to do but we have more people who are willing to give peace a chance. We broke from the rigidity of the 50s, broke the sexual mores, the cookie cutter way of looking at life. But still, that was then. I am not always part of what the young people are thinking today. They have totally different concerns and I sometimes find that hard.

And yet, friends tell me that I am in the zeitgeist by the nature of being a global spirit. With the internet, the world has become one. And that is how I live. I reside on three different continents – Australia with my husband, India with my practice and music and the USA with my family and production of my music. All these places have elements that are deep in my soul. I love my life. The rest is location.

Many people saw hippies as space cadets. I just laugh. We were the ones who did believe in peace and love and look at what happened. One world in the making. A Black President. And more and more people seeking spirituality. The 'money world' seems to be falling apart and once again grass roots activities, now through the internet, are affecting change.

Hippies rule, I say, and much of what we did is still relevant. But mostly what rules is living the life you believe in and giving it your all. Your discipline, generosity and belief. Go out and live the life you are meant to live, on your terms which should be the terms of making other people's lives easier and enjoying every second of this very beautiful planet we are gracing time with. If you do that, all I can say is:

Aum Shanti Aum.

GLOSSARY

16th Street Baptist Church bombing

The 16th Street Baptist Church bombing was an act of terrorism and white supremacy. The date was September 15, 1963, four members of the KKK planted dynamite on the steps on the 16th Street Baptist Church in Birmingham, Alabama the explosion killed four girls attending Sunday school and injured 22 members. Described by *Dr. Martin Luther King Jr.* as "one of the most vicious and tragic crimes ever perpetrated against humanity." Those responsible were each convicted of illegally possessing and transporting dynamite. They each received a $1,000 fine and a suspended six-month jail sentence. The bombing marked a turning point in the United States 1960s *Civil Rights Movement* and contribut ed to the support of the passage of the Civil Rights Act of 1964.

African-American Civil Rights Movement

The African-American Civil Rights Movement or 1960's Civil Rights Movement. The largest human rights movement in the United States to end racial discrimination against Blacks. The goal was to bring an end to racial segregation and racial discrimination and provide legal protection to all citizens as per the Constitution of the US federal law.

Alice Coltrane

Alice Coltrane or Swamini Turiyasangitnanda, (1937–2007), was an American jazz pianist, organist, harpist and composer, and the second wife of jazz saxophonist and composer John Coltrane. One of the few harpists in the history of jazz, she recorded many albums as a bandleader, beginning in the late 1960s and early 1970s for Impulse! Records and Universal Distribution.

Coltrane was a devotee of the Indian guru *Sathya Sai Baba*. In 1972, she moved to California, where she established the *Vedantic* Center in 1975. By the late 1970s she had changed her name to Turiyasangitananda. Coltrane was the spiritual

155

director, or Swamini, of Shanti Anantam Ashram established in 1983 near Malibu, California.

AME Church	The African Methodist Episcopal, AME Church was founded, in 1816 by Rev. Richard Allen in Philadelphia, Pennsylvania. The AME Church grew out of the Free African Society (FAS), which was established in Philadelphia in 1787. The Mission of the African Methodist Episcopal Church is to minister to the spiritual development of all people.
Aretha Louise Franklin	Aretha Louise Franklin, born March 25, 1942 is an American singer and musician. Franklin began her career singing gospel at her father, the Reverend C L Franklin's church as a child. Franklin has won a total of 18 Grammy Awards and is one of the best-selling female artists of all time, having sold over 75-million records worldwide. Franklin has been honored throughout her career including a 1987 induction into the *Rock and Roll Hall of Fame*, in which she became the first female performer to be inducted. She was inducted to the UK Music Hall of Fame in 2005. In August 2012, Franklin was inducted into the GMA Gospel Music Hall of Fame. Franklin is listed in at least two all-time lists on 'Rolling Stone' magazine, including the 100 Greatest Artists of All Time, in which she placed number 9, and the 100 Greatest Singers of All Time in which she was placed number 1.
Ashram	Traditionally, in India a spiritual hermitage or a monastery. Additionally, today the term ashram often denotes a locus of Hindu cultural activity such as yoga, music study or religious instruction, similar to a studio, yeshiva, i'tikāf or *dojo*.
Athletic scholarship	An Athletic scholarship is a form of scholarship to attend a college or university.
Ayurveda	Ayurveda, which literally means the science of life (Ayur = Life, Veda = Science), *Ayurveda* is an ancient medical science which was developed in India thousands of years ago.

Berry Gordy Jr.	Berry Gordy Jr. born 1929 is an American record producer, and songwriter. He is best known as the founder of the Motown record label, as well as its many subsidiaries.
Bhagavad Gita	The Bhagavad Gita has been highly praised; the *Gitas'*emphasis on selfless service was a prime source of inspiration for Gandhi. It is a 700-verse Hindu scripture that is part of the Hindu epic *Mahabharata. Gandhi* referred to the *Gita* as his "spiritual dictionary."
Bill Withers	William Harrison 'Bill' Withers Jr. born July 4, 1938 is an American singer-songwriter and musician, who won the Grammy Award for the Best R&B Song *'Ain't No Sunshine.'* in 2015; he will be inducted into the Rock and Roll Hall of Fame.
Billie Holiday (1915-1959)	An American jazz singer and songwriter prominent in the 1940s and 50's, who recorded extensively for 4 record labels. Nicknamed 'Lady Day' by her friend and musical partner Lester Young, influenced by Louis Armstrong and singer Bessie Smith. Billie Holiday was posthumously inducted into the Grammy Hall of Fame. *Jazz at the Philharmonic* is a great song collection that captures Holiday at her very best.
Black Power	Black Power is a political slogan and a name for various associated ideologies aimed at achieving self-determination for people of African-Black descent. It is used by African-Americans in the United States. The movement was prominent in the late 1960s and early 1970s, emphasizing racial pride and the creation of black political and cultural institutions to nurture and promote black collective interests and advance black values. Black Power expresses a range of political goals, from defense against racial oppression, to the establishment of social institutions and a self-sufficient economy. The earliest known usage of the term is found in a 1954 book by Richard Wright entitled *Black Power*.
Cambridge	Cambridge is a city in Middlesex County, Massachusetts,

United States, in the Boston metropolitan area, situated directly north of the city of Boston proper and across the Charles River. It was named in honor of the University of Cambridge in England, and is home to two of the world's most prominent universities, Harvard University and the Massachusetts Institute of Technology. Cam-bridge has also been home to Radcliffe College, once one of the leading colleges for women in the United States before it merged with Harvard.

Candy Striper

This name is derived from the red-and-white striped jumpers that female hospital volunteers traditionally wore.

Carnegie Hall

A 3,671 seat concert venue in Midtown Manhattan in New York City, next to Central Park. Built in 1891, it is in one of the most prestigious venues in the world for both classical music and popular music, all of whom made celebrated live recordings of their concerts there. Sissieretta Jones became the first African-American to sing at the Music Hall (renamed Carnegie Hall the following year), June 15 1892.

Chakras

Chakras are those energy centers through which the Cosmic energy flows into the human body. The practice of "Yoga in Daily Life" can awaken these centers, which are manifest in each and every person.

Chamundi Hills

Chamundi Hills 13 km east of Mysore, has an average elevation of 1,000 meters (3,300 ft) and is regarded as a sacred place. Named after goddess Chamunda, the Chamundeshwari Temple is on the top of the main hill. The main hill itself features an ancient stone stairway of 1,008 steps leading to its summit. Approximately halfway to the summit is the statue of Nandi Bull, the mount and gatekeeper of god Shiva.

Charles Burnham

Charles Burnham born 1950, also known as Charlie Burnham, is an American violinist and composer. He has a unique highly imaginative style that crosses genres, including bluegrass, delta punk, free, jazz, blues, classical and chamber jazz. He often performs with a *wah-wah* pedal. He initially became renowned for his work on James 'Blood' Ulmer's Odyssey album. The musicians on that album later performed and recorded as Odyssey The Band, sometimes known as The Odyssey Band. He was also a member of the String Trio of New York.

Co-op schools
A co-operative education that integrates classroom study with professional experience on seven continents.

Counter-culture
A counter-culture is a sub-culture whose values and norms of behavior differ substantially from main stream society. At times the movement divided the population.

Crips & Bloods
The Crips are primarily an African-American gang. They were founded in Los Angeles, California in 1969. The Bloods are a primarily, though not exclusively, African-American street gang founded in Los Angeles, California. They are identified by the red color worn by their members and by particular gang symbols, including distinctive hand signs.

Curtis Lee Mayfield
Curtis Lee Mayfield, (1942–1999), was an African-American soul, R&B and funk singer-songwriter, guitarist, and record producer, who was one of the most influential musicians behind soul and politically conscious African-American music. He first achieved success and recognition with the *Impressions* during the Civil Rights Movement of the late 1950s and 1960s, and later worked as a solo artist.

Dhyanyogi
Shri Dhyanyogi Madhusudandas (1878-1984), was an Indian sage born in Bihar. His disciples include Shri Anandi Ma and Omdasji Maharaj. He was a master of Kundalini Maha Yoga.

Drum Major Instinct
Martin Luther King's "Drum Major Instinct" sermon, given on February 4, 1968, two months before his assassination was an adaptation of the 1952 homily "Drum Major Instincts" by J. Wallace Hamilton, a well-known liberal white Methodist preacher. King encouraged his congregation to seek greatness, but to do so through service and love. King concluded the

sermon by imagining his own funeral, downplaying his famous achievements and emphasizing his heart to do right. Both men tell the biblical story of James and John, who ask Jesus for the most prominent seats in heaven. At the core of their desire was a "drum major instinct—a desire to be out front, a desire to lead the parade."

Emancipation Proclamation

The Emancipation Proclamation was a presidential proclamation and executive order issued by President Abraham Lincoln on January 1, 1863. It proclaimed the freedom of slaves in the ten states that were still in rebellion and applied to more than 3 million of the 4 million slaves. The Proclamation was based on the president's constitutional authority as commander in chief of the armed forces; it was not a law passed by Congress. The goal was to reunite the Union. *Dr. Martin Luther King Jr.* often referred to the Emancipation Proclamation in his many speeches and work for Civil Rights.

Emmett Louis Till

African-American teenager who was murdered in Mississippi at the age of 14 after reportedly whistling at a white woman. Till's murder is one of the pivotal events in the organizing of the civil rights movement. Emmett Till was from Chicago, Illinois, and was visiting relatives in Money, Mississippi. He spoke to the 21 year old female store clerk of a small grocery store there. Nights later, the husband and his half-brothers went to Till's great-uncle's house. They took Till away to a barn, where they beat him before shooting him through the head and disposing of his body in the river, weighting it with a 70 pound (32 kg) cotton gin fan tied around his neck with barbed wire. Three days later, Till's body was discovered and retrieved from the river. In September 1955, the accused men were acquitted of Till's kidnapping and murder, protected against double jeopardy. In an interview with Look magazine, the two men accused, admitted that they killed Till.

Etta James	Born Jamesetta Hawkins (1938–2012) Etta James was an American singer. Her style spanned a variety of music genres including blues, R&B, soul, rock and roll, jazz and gospel. James is regarded as having bridged the gap between rhythm and blues and rock and roll, and was the winner of six Grammys and 17 Blues Music Awards. She was inducted into the Rock and Roll Hall of Fame in 1993, the Blues Hall of Fame in 2001, and the Grammy Hall of Fame in both 1999 and 2008. 'Rolling Stone' ranked James number 22 on their list of the 100 Greatest Singers of All Time and number 62 on the list of the 100 Greatest Artists. Though she wasn't the first singer to perform it, Etta James made the smoldering ballad *'At Last'* her signature song since it became a hit for her in 1961.
Fat back	Is a cut of meat from pork, a traditional part of southern US cuisine and soul food.
Garden City of India	Bangalore's reputation as the Garden City of India began in 1927 with the Silver Jubilee celebrations of the rule of Krishnaraja Wodeyar IV.
GED	General Educational Development tests are a group of four subject tests which, when passed, certify that the student has American or Canadian high school-level academic skills.
Gilbert 'Gil' Scott-Heron	Gilbert 'Gil' Scott-Heron 1949–2011, was an American soul and jazz poet, musician and author, known primarily for his work as a spoken word performer in the 1970's and 80's. His collaborative efforts with musician Brian Jackson featured a musical fusion of jazz, blues, and soul, as well as lyrical content concerning social and political issues of the time, delivered in both rapping and melismatic vocal styles by Scott-Heron. His own term for himself was 'bluesologist', which he defined as "a scientist who is concerned with the origin of the blues." His music, most notably on Pieces of a Man and Winter in America in the early 1970's, influenced and helped

engender later African-American music genres such as hip hop and neo-soul.

Gladys Knight   Gladys Maria Knight born May 28, 1944 is an American recording artist, songwriter. A four-time Grammy Award-winner she is best known for the hits she recorded during the 1960's and 1970's, for both the Motown and Buddha Records labels, with her group Gladys Knight & the Pips, which also included her brother and her cousins. In 1996, Gladys Knight & the Pips were inducted into the Rock and Roll Hall of Fame. One year before, Knight had received a star on the Hollywood Walk of Fame. In 2007, Knight received the Society of Singers ELLA Award, at which time she was declared the "Empress of Soul". She is listed on Rolling Stone's list of the Greatest Singers of All Time.

Good ol' boys   Good ol' boys or, a man or older boy from the South, in this case the stereotypical redneck or hick.

Gramoph-one/pho-nograph   Record or vinyl record, commonly known as a 'record', generally described by their diameter in inches (12", 10", 7"), the rotational speed in rpm at which they are played (16⅔, 33⅓, 45, 78) hence; 78's.

Grass-roots   Grass-roots movement can be a political movement that is driven by a community's desire to take on community issues. Grassroots movements are often at the local level, as many volunteers in the community give their time to support the community local party.

Haight-Ashbury   Haight-Ashbury is a district of San Francisco, California, named for the intersection of Haight and Ashbury streets. It is also called 'The Haight,' home of the hippie counter culture.

Hatha Yoga   The word hatha means willful or forceful. Hatha yoga refers to a set of physical exercises (known as asanas or postures), and sequences of asanas, designed to align your skin, muscles, and bones. The postures are also designed to open the many channels of the body - especially the main channel, the spine—so that energy can flow freely.

Head Shop   A head shop is a retail outlet specializing in tobacco paraphernalia used for consumption of tobacco, legal highs, legal party powders and New Age herbs as well as counterculture art, magazines, music, clothing and home decor; some head shops also sell oddities, such as antique walking sticks. Sources cite the Psychedelic Shop on Haight Street in San Francisco as the first head shop in the United States.

Hindu Temple Society of North America   The Hindu Temple Society of North America, representing *Sri Maha Vallabha Ganapati Devasthanam*, at 45-57 Bowne Street, Flushing, Queens, in New York City, was the very first of the traditional Hindu temples in the USA. It is popularly referred to as the Ganesh Temple, Flushing, since the main deity is Lord Ganesh. The temple architecture and the rituals follow the South Indian tradition.

Hinduism   Hinduism is the dominant religion of the Indian subcontinent. It comprises three major traditions, Shaivism, Vaishnavism and Shaktism, whose followers considered Shiva, Vishnu and Shakti also called Devi, to be the supreme deity respectively. Most of the other deities were either related to them or different forms (incarnations) of these deities. Hinduism has been called the "oldest religion" in the world and many practitioners refer to Hinduism as "the eternal law". (*Sanātana Dharma*). Within Hinduism, a large number of personal gods (Ishvaras) are worshipped as murtis. These beings are significantly powerful entities known as devas. The exact nature of belief in regard to each deity varies between differing Hindu denominations and philosophies.

Hindustan Ambassador   The Hindustan Ambassador was an automobile manufactured by Hindustan Motors of India and despite its British origins, is considered as a definitive Indian car and is fondly called 'The king of Indian roads'.

HIV/AIDS Human immunodeficiency virus infection and acquired immune deficiency syndrome, is a spectrum of conditions caused by infection with the human immunodeficiency virus. The disease has had a great impact on society, both as an illness and as a source of discrimination.

Homeless shelters Homeless shelters are temporary residences for homeless people which seek to protect vulnerable populations from the often devastating effects of homelessness. Homeless shelters tend to be a "one-size-fits-all" model, but there is frequently a separate shelter system for families and for youth.

Iyengar Way Yoga: The Iyengar Way by Silva, Mira and Shyam Metha published in 1990. A comprehensive, practical, and authoritative guide to the method developed by BKS Iyengar. 100 key postures with detailed step-by-step instructions and photographs.

James Cleveland The Rev Dr James Edward Cleveland (1931-1991), was a gospel singer, musician, and composer. Known as the King of Gospel music. Throughout his career, Cleveland appeared on hundreds of recordings, won four Grammy Awards, and received a star along the Hollywood Walk of Fame.

James 'Blood' Ulmer James 'Blood' Ulmer born, 1940 is an American jazz, free funk and blues guitarist and singer. Ulmer plays a semi-acoustic guitar. His distinctive guitar sound has been described as 'jagged' and 'stinging'. Ulmer's singing has been called 'raggedly soulful'.

Jessye Mae Norman Jessye Mae Norman born September 15, 1945 is an African-American Grammy award-winning opera singer and recitalist. A dramatic soprano, Norman was greatly inspired by opera greats Marian Anderson and Leontyne Price. She Attended Howard University, became a professional soloist, moved to Europe to established herself and won contracts with prestigious opera houses. Norman lived in and toured Europe for many years. Norman has been inducted into the Georgia

Music Hall of Fame and is a Spingarn Medalist. Apart from receiving several honorary doctorates and other awards, she has also received the Grammy Lifetime Achievement Award, the National Medal of Arts and is a member of the British Royal Academy of Music.

John V. Lindsay
John V. Lindsay (1921–2000), was an American politician, lawyer and broadcaster who was a U.S. congressman, mayor of New York City, candidate for U.S. president and regular guest host of *Good Morning America*. Well known for spending a great deal of time in New York City's inner city neighborhoods Lindsay traveled directly into Harlem, telling black residents that he regretted King's death and was working against poverty, assured the community he is known for walking the streets of Bedford-Stuyvesant and Harlem, when these neighborhoods were doing poorly economically.

Journey to the One
Journey to the One is a double album led by saxophonist Pharoah Sanders.

Korunta
The Yoga Korunta is an ancient Sanskrit text on yoga by Vamana Rishi and allegedly discovered by Tirumalai Krishnamacharya in the National Archives of India in the early 20th century. The text is said to have described several lists of many different asana groupings, as well as highly original teachings on vinyasa, drishti, bandhas, mudras and general teachings.

The name *Yoga Korunta* is the Tamilized pronunciation of the Sanskrit words *Yoga grantha*, meaning "book about yoga."

KKK - three cousins
The KKK - three cousins or the Klan Three - white supremacy movements in the United States. The group first organized in 1860 and committed violent acts against African Americans. They were quiet for a few years and regrouped in the 20s. During this time they took on the famous uniform white

sheets with holes for the eyes nose and mouth. They went underground for a while then resurfaced with the Civil Rights movement, strongly opposing the progress of people of color. They are considered white right wing supremacists. They made alliances with Southern police departments or with governor's offices. Several members of KKK groups were convicted of murder in the deaths of civil rights workers and children, though most members of the KKK saw themselves as holding to American values and Christian morality.

Krishnama-charya
Tirumalai Krishnamacharya (1888–1989), was an Indian Yoga teacher, *ayurvedic* healer and scholar. Often referred to as "The Father of Modern Yoga," *Krishnamacharya* is widely regarded as one of the most influential yoga teachers of the 20th century and is credited with the revival of hatha yoga.

Kukkara-halli Lake
Kukkarahalli Lake is spread over 58 hectares with a shoreline of roughly five kilometers of the sprawling campus of the University of Mysore. This lake is home to more than 180 species of birds, some of them aquatic. During the migratory season the lake plays host to a variety of winged visitors, some from as far as Siberia. The birds found in the lake are Spot-billed Pelicans, Little Cormorant, Painted Storks, Open-bill Storks, Eurasian Spoonbills, Black-crowned Night Herons and Oriental Darters. Bird life International has included Kukkarahalli Lake in the list of 38 Important Bird Areas (IBAs) in Karnataka.

Kundalini
Kundalini comes from yogic philosophy as a form of *shakti* or 'corporeal energy' lying 'coiled' at the base of the spine. Kundalini awakening involves the Kundalini physically moving up the central channel to reach within the Sahasrara Chakra at the top of the head.

Kwame Touré
Kwame Touré, once known as Stokely Carmichael (1941–1998), was a Trinidadian-American activist active in the 1960's Civil Rights Movement and later, the global Pan-African

movement. Growing up in the United States from the age of eleven, he graduated from Howard University. He rose to prominence in the civil rights and Black Power movements, first as a leader of the Student Nonviolent Coordinating Committee (SNCC), later as the "Honorary Prime Minister" of the Black Panther Party, and finally as a leader of the All-African People's Revolutionary Party.

Ladies holiday	In Ashtanga Yoga practice originally, five days rest had to be taken during women's cycle.
Langston University	Is a public university founded in 1897. It was known as the Oklahoma Colored Agricultural University. Langston University was created as a result of the second Morrill Act in 1890, a law that required states with land-grant colleges, such as Oklahoma State University, to either admit African-Americans, or provide an alternative school for them to attend, as a condition of receiving federal funds.
Light On Yoga	Light On Yoga known as the Bible of the definitive guide to the philosophy and practice of Yoga—the ancient healing discipline for body and mind.
Lunch counter sit-in	In October 1960, Martin Luther King was arrested along with around 280 students because of his participation in nonviolent efforts to integrate lunch counters in Atlanta, Georgia. The students initiating the lunch counter sit-in and asked him to join in. Two days later the charges were dropped but King was held for violating probation for an earlier traffic offense and transferred to Reidsville State Prison. Senator Robert Kennedy called Georgia governor S. Ernest Vandiver and Judge Oscar Mitchell seeking King's release and bail.
Maha-bharata	Mahabharata is one of the two Sanskrit epics of ancient India, the other being *Ramayana*.
Mahalia Jackson	Mahalia Jackson (1911–1972), "The Queen of Gospel Music," was an American gospel singer possessing a powerful contralto voice. She is still considered as one of the most important

influential voices of all time and praised the world over. She was a civil rights activist and recorded 30 albums. She was the first gospel singer to sing at Carnegie hall. She encouraged Dr. MLK to recite his famous I have a Dream speech. Mahalia Jackson sang "Take My Hand Precious Lord" after Dr. King was assassinated.

Mahatma Gandhi	Mahatma Gandhi (1869 –1948), also known as Bapu, was the pre-eminent leader of Indian independence movement in British-ruled India. Employing nonviolent civil disobedience, Gandhi led India to independence and inspired movements for civil rights and freedom across the world.
Mantra	Mantra are sacred sounds. Early mantras were composed in vedic times by Hindus in India. Mantra practice dates back some 3,000 years and was used by Hindus, Buddhists, Jains and Sikhs. They are believed to transform energy. They are sound based and often used prior to meditation. Mantras vary according to the school of philosophy they represent. They are often found in Hindu Text. The most common mantra is Aum.
March on Washington "I Have a Dream"	The March on Washington was one of the largest political rallies for human rights in United States history on Wednesday, August 28, 1963. Martin Luther King Jr, standing in front of the Lincoln Memorial, delivered his historic "I Have a Dream" speech in which he called for an end to racism. The march is credited with helping to pass the Civil Rights Act (1964) and preceded the Selma Voting Rights Movement which led to the passage of the Voting Rights Act (1965).
Melukote	Melukote, Karnataka, in southern India, is one of the sacred places in Karnataka. It is built on rocky hills, known as Yadugiri, Yaadavagiri and Yadushailadweepa, overlooking the Cauvery valley. Melukote is about 51 km (32 miles) from Mysore and 133 km (83 mi) from Bangalore. Melukote is the location of the Cheluvanarayana Swamy Temple, with a

collection of crowns and jewels which are brought to the temple for the annual celebration. On the top of the hill is the temple of Yoganarasimha. Many more shrines and ponds are located in the town. Melukote is home to the Academy of Sanskrit Research, which has collected thousands of manuscripts.

Metropole Hotel	The Metropole Hotel built by the Maharaja of Mysore in 1920 for his distinguished British guests. It was closed for renovation for 10 years in 1994 and is now a four star grand heritage hotel. Steeped in the history and culture of a charming old world Mysore. It features imperial arches, imposing pillars and ornate corridors.
MIT	MIT is often cited as among the world's top universities. The *Massachusetts Institute of Technology (MIT)* is a private research university in Cambridge, Massachusetts. Founded in 1861 in response to the increasing industrialization of the United States, MIT has five schools and one college which contain a total of 32 departments. It is traditionally known for research and education in the physical sciences and engineering, and more recently in biology, economics, linguistics and management as well.
Motown	Motown is an American record company founded by Berry Gordy Jr on January 12, 1959 in Detroit, Michigan; the name, a blending of *motor* and *town*, is also a nickname for Detroit. Motown played an important role in the racial integration of popular music as an African American-owned record label which achieved significant crossover success.
Mula Bhanda	Means 'root' or 'lock' and Bandha means posture or joining together. Mula Bandha is one of the three 'body locks' in Yoga that, when activated—or when the muscles of the perineum are locked—allows the energy in the *pranic* body to 'unlock' and be redirected upwards creating a light body.

| Mysuru/ | Mysuru, is the third largest city in the state of Karnataka, |
| Mysore | India, which served as the capital city of Mysore Princely |

Mysuru/ Mysore   Mysuru, is the third largest city in the state of Karnataka, India, which served as the capital city of Mysore Princely Kingdom (Kingdom of Mysore) for nearly six centuries, from 1399 until 1947. Located at the base of the *Chamundi Hills* about 146km (91mi) southwest of the state capital Bangalore, it is spread across an area of 128km^2 (50mi^2). According to the provisional results of the 2011 national census of India, the population of Mysore is 887,446. The Kingdom of Mysore was ruled by the Wodeyar dynasty, except for a brief period in the late 18th century when Hyder Ali and Tipu Sultan were in power. Patrons of art and culture, the Wodeyars contributed significantly to the cultural growth of the city. The cultural ambience and achievements of Mysore earned it the sobriquet *Cultural capital of South Karnataka*. Mysore is noted for its palaces, including the Mysore Palace, and for the festivities that take place during the *Dasara* festival when the city receives a large number of tourists. It lends its name to the Mysore style of painting, the sweet dish *Mysore Pak*, the *Mysore Peta* (a traditional silk turban) and the garment known as the Mysore silk sari. In the famed Jaganmohan Palace there was a Yoga Shala, where the great Sage and Yoga Master, *Krishnamacharya* taught both *Pattabhi Jois* and *BKS Iyengar*. They both consequently intensified Yoga practice and introduced it to the modern world stage, in a more inclusive method than the Yoga that *Swami Vivekananda* had brought to the West a generation before.

Namaskar   In Hinduism it means "I bow to the divine in you". Namaste or Namaskar is used as a respectful form of greeting,

National Association for the Advancement of Colored   The National Association for the Advancement of Colored People, NAACP, is an organization formed in 1909. Its mission is "to ensure the political, educational, social, and economic equality of rights of all persons and to eliminate racial hatred and racial discrimination." The NAACP seeks to remove all barriers of racial discrimination through the

People	democratic processes.
National Urban League (NUL)	The NUL is the oldest and largest community-based civil rights organization of its kind in the US. It is based in New York City and advocates on behalf of African-Americans in the struggle against racial discrimination in the United States.
Native Americans	Indigenous people who live within the boundaries of the present-day United States, including the indigenous peoples of Alaska and Hawaii.
Nina Simone	Nina Simone (1933–2003) was an American singer, songwriter, pianist, arranger, and civil rights activist. She worked in a broad range of musical styles including classical, jazz, blues, folk, R&B, gospel and pop. Over the length of her career Simone recorded more than 40 albums.
No Coloreds Allowed	Signs often displayed the racial divide and the racial segregation in the United States. This included the segregation of facilities, services, and opportunities such as housing, medical care, education, employment, and transportation along racial lines. These signs also showed up in eating establishment's theaters restrooms and of course in public transportation. The services and facilities reserved for African-Americans were almost always of lower quality than those reserved for whites; for example, most African-American schools received less public funding per student than nearby white schools.
Operation Shanti	Operation Shanti (Sanskrit word meaning peace, calmness) a San Francisco, based non-profit organization, was formally established in 2005 to help the poorest and neediest gain status and their rightful place in their societies.
Pattabhi Jois	Sri K. Pattabhi Jois (1915–2009), was a world renowned Indian yoga teacher Yoga Guru. He introduced the traditional ancient practice of Ashtanga Yoga to the Western World.

Jois's father was an astrologer, priest, and landholder. From the age of 5, he was instructed in Sanskrit and rituals by his father. In 1927, at the age of 12, Jois attended a lecture and demonstration at the Jubilee Hall in Hassan by *T Krishnamacharya* and became his student the very next day. For two years Jois remained in Kowshika and practiced with Krishnamacharya every day. In 1948 Jois established the Ashtanga Yoga Research Institute (now known as the Shri K Pattabhi Jois Ashtanga Yoga Institute) in Mysore. He held a teaching position in yoga at the Sanskrit College of Maharaja from 1937 to 1973, becoming *vidwan* (professor) in 1956, as well as being Honorary Professor of Yoga at the Government College of Indian Medicine from 1976 to 1978. He taught there until 1973, when he left to devote himself fully to teach yoga at his yoga shala. He had studied texts such as the *Patañjali Yoga Darśana*, *Haṭha Yoga Pradīpikā*, *Yoga Yajñavalkya* and the *Upaniṣads*, and in 1948, he established the Ashtanga Yoga Research Institute at their new home Lakshmipuram. Jois continued to teach at the Ashtanga Yoga Research Institute in Mysore, with his only daughter Saraswathi Rangaswamy (born in 1941) and his grandson Sharath (born in 1971), until May 18, 2009, when he died aged 93.

Peyote Is a small, spineless cactus with psychoactive alkaloids, particularly mescaline, native to southwestern Texas and Mexico, used in ceremonies by Native Americans for spiritual purposes.

Pharaoh Sanders Pharoah Sanders, born October 13, 1940, is a Grammy Award-winning American jazz saxophonist. Saxophonist Ornette Coleman once described him as "probably the best tenor player in the world." Emerging from John Coltrane's groups of the mid-1960s Sanders is known for his over-blowing, harmonic, and multi-phonic techniques on the saxophone, as well as his use of "sheets of sound." Sanders is an important figure in the develop-ment of free jazz. *Albert Ayler* famously said: "Trane was the Father, Pharaoh was the Son, I am the Holy Ghost." Sanders was strongly influenced by his collaboration with Coltrane. Spiritual elements such as the chanting in *Om* would later show up in many of Sanders' own works. Sanders would also go on to produce much free jazz. In the 1970's, Sanders pursued his own recordings and continued to work with the likes of Alice Coltrane on her *Journey In Satchidananda* album. Most of Sanders' best-selling works were made in the late 1960's and early 1970's for Impulse Records, including the 30-minute wave-on-wave of free jazz "The Creator has a Master Plan" from the album *Karma*.

Prana

Prana is the Sanskrit word for "life force"; in yoga, Indian medicine, and martial arts, the term refers to a cosmic energy believed to come from the sun and connecting the elements of the universe. The universal principle of energy or force, responsible for the body's life, heat and maintenance, prana is the sum total of all energy that is manifest in the universe.

Pranic

Pranic Healing - transforming how the body process energy to balance the Prana in the body. Prana is the Sanskrit word for "life force."

Protest movements

Protest movements in the1960's

- the civil rights movement,
- the student movement,
- the anti-Vietnam War movement,
- the women's movement,
- the gay rights movement, and
- the environmental movement.

Just to name a few of the organizations that changed government policy in America and life in America changed forever. The American people began to ask questions: Why are things separate and unequal? Why are the funds that go into the white community schools more than the funds that go into black community schools?. Why must our children go to separate schools?. Why are women paid less than men for the same job?. Should males be drafted at age 18 but not vote till age 21. Supporters took direct action, there were public marches and demonstrations there were sit-in petitions signed. People worked for hours to make a change to make a better more just society for everyone.

Public Broad-casting Service   The Public Broadcasting Service is an American public broadcaster and television program distributor. Headquartered in Arlington, Virginia, PBS is an independently operated non-profit organization and is the most prominent provider of television programs to public television stations in the United States.

Quarter tone   A quarter tone is a pitch halfway between the usual notes of a chronicle scale.

Raja   Literally means king. Raja Yoga thus, refers to best of Yoga.

Ray Carlos Nakai   Ray Carlos Nakai was born in Flagstaff, Arizona on April 16, 1946 and now resides in Tucson, Arizona. He is a Native American of Navajo and Ute heritage who began his musical career as a freshman at Northern Arizona University studying brass instruments and playing in the NAU marching band.

Richard Freeman   Richard Freeman has been a student of yoga since 1968. He has spent nearly twelve years in Asia studying various traditions.

Robert F. Kennedy   Robert F. Kennedy's speech on the assassination of *Martin Luther King Jr* was given on April 4, 1968 in Indianapolis, Indiana. Kennedy, the United States senator from New York, was campaigning to earn the 1968 Democratic presidential nomination when he learned that King had been assassinated in Memphis, Tennessee. Earlier that day Kennedy had spoken at the University of Notre Dame in South Bend and at Ball State University in Muncie, Indiana. Before boarding a plane to attend campaign rallies in Indianapolis, Kennedy learned that King had been shot. When he arrived, Kennedy was informed that King had died. Despite fears of riots and concerns for his safety, Kennedy went ahead with plans to attend a rally at 17th and Broadway in the heart of Indianapolis' African-American ghetto. That evening Kennedy addressed the crowd, many of whom had not heard about King's assassination. Instead of the rousing campaign speech they expected, Kennedy offered brief, impassioned remarks for peace that is considered to be one of the great public addresses of the modern era.

Rudra Hindu prayer or hymn dedicated to Rudra, an epithet of Shiva. Literally means that "Fire comes from the Bowels of the earth spreading God's grace all over the world".

Sādhu In Hinduism, a sādhu - Sanskrit for, "good; good man, holy man" - is a religious ascetic or holy person. Although the vast majority of sādhus are yogīs, not all yogīs are sādhus . The sādhu is solely dedicated to achieving moksa (liberation), the fourth and final aśrama (stage of life), through meditation and contemplation of Brahman. Sādhus often wear saffron-coloured clothing, symbolising their sanyāsa (renunciation). This way of life is open to women; the female form of the word is sādhvī.

Sarah Lois Vaughan Sarah Lois Vaughan (1924–1990), was an American jazz singer. Nicknamed 'Sassy' Sarah Vaughan, she was a Grammy Award winner. The National Endowment for the Arts and received the "highest honor in jazz", the NEA Jazz Masters Award, in 1989.

Sarus Cranes Sarus Cranes are considered sacred and the birds are traditionally left unharmed, and in many areas they are unafraid of humans. The species is venerated in India and legend has it that the poet Valmiki cursed a hunter for killing a Sarus Crane and was then inspired to write the epic Ramayana. The species was a close contender to the Indian peafowl as the national bird of India. Among the Gondi people, the tribes classified as "five-god worshippers" consider the Sarus Crane as sacred. The meat of the Sarus was considered taboo in ancient Hindu scriptures. It is widely believed that the Sarus pairs for life and that death of one partner leads to the other pining to death. They are a symbol of marital virtue and in parts of Gujarat it is a custom to take a newlywed couple to see a pair of Sarus Cranes.

SAT   The Scholastic Aptitude Test is a standardized test widely used for college admissions in the United States.

Satchi-danananda   Swami Satchidananda Saraswati (1914-2002), born as C K Ramaswamy Gounder, was an Indian religious teacher, spiritual master and yoga adept, who gained fame and following in the West.

Selma   On 25 March 1965, *Martin Luther King* led thousands of nonviolent demonstrators to the steps of the capitol in Montgomery, Alabama, after a 5-day, 54-mile march from Selma, Alabama, where local African-Americans, the Student Nonviolent Coordinating Committee (SNCC) and the Southern Christian Leadership Conference (SCLC) had been campaigning for voting rights.

Shala   Is a house in Hindi.

Shamans   Altered states of consciousness, a person with access to the spiritual world.

Shirley Caesar   Shirley Caesar (born in 1938), is an American Gospel music singer, songwriter and recording artist whose career has spanned over six decades. A multi-award winning artist, with eleven Grammy Awards and seven Dove Awards to her credit, she is known as the *"First Lady of Gospel Music."*

Speaking in tongues	Glossolalia often understood as speaking in tongues, Human Sounds that are made during a transcendental or altered state of consciousness. Some say that it is a religious practice and consider it as a part of a sacred language.
Spirituals (or Negro spirituals)	Are religious (generally Christian) songs that were created by African slaves that tell the stories of life during that time in the United States. They were (unison) songs originally, but today are harmonized choral arrangements. A lot of the decoding and recoding of words came during this unison chanting and singing.
Strange Fruit	Strange Fruit is a poem written by American writer, teacher and songwriter *Abel Meeropol*. First published under the title of 'Bitter Fruit' A protest against lynchings. He often used others to set his poems to music, but he set the music himself to 'Strange Fruit'. His protest song gained a certain success in and around New York. Meeropol, his wife and black vocalist Laura Duncan performed it at Madison Square Garden. Holiday first performed the song in 1939 at Cafe Society in Greenwich Village, New York's first integrated nightclub. She performed the piece in a very dramatic way with the room in darkness and the spotlight on her face; it has been written that she went into either prayer or a deep trance.
Student Nonviolent Coordinating Committee	The Student Nonviolent Coordinating Committee (SNCC) was one of the most important organizations of the American Civil Rights Movement in the 1960's. Emerging from a student meeting organized by Ella Baker held at Shaw University in April 1960, SNCC grew into a large organization. Many unpaid volunteers worked with SNCC on projects in Mississippi, Alabama, Georgia, Arkansas and Maryland. SNCC played a major role in the sit-ins and freedom rides, a leading role in the 1963 March on Washington, Mississippi Freedom Summer, and the Mississippi Freedom Democratic Party. In the later 1960's, led

by fiery leaders such as *Stokely Carmichael*, SNCC focused on black power, and then protesting against the Vietnam War.

Sun salutations   Are a set of 12 powerful Yoga *asanas* (postures) that provide cardiovascular workout in the form of Surya (Sun) *Namaskar* (salutation).

Swami Viveka-nanda   Swami Vivekananda (1863–1902), was an Indian Hindu monk and chief disciple of the 19th-century saint Ramakrishna. He was a key figure in the introduction of the Indian philosophies of Vedanta and Yoga to the Western world.

Sweat Lodge Ceremony   Also called purification ceremony. There are several styles of sweat lodges they can be as simple as a hole dug into the ground and covered with planks or tree trunks fire and heat are used for the purification, as well as sacred ritual prayers and herbs. Usually performed by Medicine Men and Women, to repair broken spirits, and reclaim the body mind and spirit. This ceremony is performed to heal and elevate the soul.

Sylvester James Jr   Sylvester James Jr. (1947-1988), better known as Sylvester, was an American gospel R&B, disco and soul singer-songwriter, known for his flamboyant and androgynous appearance. Responsible for a string of hit singles in the late 1970's, Sylvester became known in the United States under the moniker of the *"Queen of Disco."* Sylvester developed a love for singing in his early years and sang in many gospel Pentecostal choirs. Sylvester was truly one of the greatest voices of all time and sang with the great Martha Wash, and Isoah Rhodes.

The Henry Ford   Also known as the Henry Ford Museum and Greenfield Village. Also the Edison Institute. The Ford Foundation is located in NYC its mission is to globally advance human welfare. At one time it was the largest most influential organization in the world to address and work on education human rights democracy creative arts and developing in the third world. The Ford Museum houses many historical artifacts one of those is the famous "Rosa Parks Bus," a major piece in the "Civil Rights Movement."

The Spook Who Sat by the Door

The Spook Who Sat by the Door, a spy novel by Sam Greenlee, published in 1969 is the story of Dan Freeman, the first Black CIA officer, and of the CIA's history of training persons and political groups who later used their specialized training in gathering intelligence, political subversion, and guerrilla warfare against the CIA. It is set in the late 1960s and early 1970s, in the Chicago of Mayor Richard J. Daley.

Trans-Atlantic Slave Trade Database

Is the most comprehensive analysis of shipping records over the course of the slave trade. It is estimated that between 1525 and 1866, the entire history of the slave trade to the New World, according to the records, 12.5 million Africans were shipped to the New World. 10.7 million survived the dreaded Middle Passage, disembarking in North America, the Caribbean and South America.

Upanishads

The Upanishads are a collection of texts in the Vedic Sanskrit language which contain the earliest emergence of some of the central religious concepts of Hinduism, some of which are shared with Buddhism and Jainism. The Upanishads are considered by Hindus to contain revealed truths (*Sruti*) concerning the nature of ultimate reality (*brahman*) and describing the character and form of human salvation (*moksha*).

Vedas

The Vedas (Sanskrit - knowledge) is a large body of texts originating in ancient India. Composed in Vedic Sanskrit, the texts constitute the oldest layer of Sanskrit literature and the oldest scriptures of Hinduism. Hindus consider the Vedas to be *apaurusheya*, which means "not of a man, superhuman" and "impersonal, authorless". Vedas are also called *śruti* ("what is heard") literature, distinguishing them from other religious texts, which are called *smriti*, "what is remembered". The Veda, for orthodox Indian theologians, are considered revelations, some way or other the work of the Deity. In the Hindu Epic the *Mahabharata*, the creation of Vedas is credited to Brahma.

There are four Vedas; the Rigveda, the Yajurveda, the Samaveda and the Atharvaveda. Each Veda has been sub-classified into four major text types – the Samhitas (mantras and benedictions), the Aranyakas (text on rituals, ceremonies, sacrifices and symbolic-sacrifices), the Brahmanas (commentaries on rituals, ceremonies and sacrifices), and the Upanishads (text discussing meditation, philosophy and spiritual knowledge).

We Shall Overcome   A protest song that became the main anthem for the African-American Civil Rights Movement. It is widely believed that the title and structure of the song are derived from an early gospel song, "I'll Overcome Someday," by African-American composer Charles Albert Tindley. The song "We Will Overcome" was published in the September 1948 issue of *People's Songs Bulletin* and recorded by Joe Glazer in 1950. According to the late, Pete Seeger, the song is thought to have become associated with the Civil Rights Movement from 1959, when Guy Carawan stepped in as song leader at Highlander, which was then focused on nonviolent civil rights activism. Seeger states the song quickly became the movement's unofficial anthem. Pete Seeger and other famous folksingers in the early 1960's, such as Joan Baez, sang the song at rallies, folk festivals, and concerts in the North and helped make it widely known. Since its rise to prominence, the song, and songs based on it, has been used in a variety of protests worldwide.

Yamas/ Niyamas   Yamas and Niyamas represent a series of ethical rules within Hinduism and Yoga.

Yoga Mala   Yoga Mala a book written by *Sri K. Pattabhi Jois*. In Sanskrit mala means garland. In India, there are many different kind of malas. He wrote the book in Kannada, India in 1958, and it was published in 1962, but was not published in English until 1999.

Yoga Sutras The Yoga Sutras. 196 yoga principles, were compiled around 400 CE (Christian Era) by *Patañjali* taking materials about yoga from older traditions.

Yoga Sūtras of Patañjali The Yoga Sūtras of Patañjali are 196 Indian sūtras (aphorisms) that constitute the foundational text of Ashtanga Yoga, also called *Raja Yoga*.

Yogi Bhajan Yogi Bhajan Harbhajan Singh Khalsa (1929–2004), also known as *Yogi Bhajan* and *Siri Singh Sahib*, was an influential spiritual leader and entrepreneur who introduced *Kundalini Yoga* to the United States. He was the spiritual director of the 3HO - Healthy, Happy, Holy Organization - Foundation. He is one of the many credited with bringing Yoga to the masses in the west. Yogi Bhajan's message of no drugs, family values and healthy living was widely popular, and many of the media stories were positive, serving not only to educate the public, but also to publicize the work of the 3HO Foundation.

Thanks Wikipedia